Your First Cut

A Step-by-Step Guide to Getting There

by

Jerry Vandiver and Gracie Hollombe

MISSION STATEMENT

This workbook is designed to guide, encourage and enable the aspiring, serious songwriter toward achieving the goal of acquiring his or her first cut.

CONTENTS

CAST OF CHARACTERS

As it is in any writing endeavor, it is never done alone. There have been many people in our camp encouraging us, supporting us, offering invaluable advice and feedback.

To the many songwriters who have walked this path and to those who graciously allowed us to interview them: Pat Alger, Kent Blazy, Jason Blume, Steve Bogard, Bruce Channel, Roxie Dean, Danny Flowers, Liz Hengber, Jon Ims, Steven Dale Jones, Kirsti Manna, Layng Martine, Jr., Wood Newton, Bob Regan, Arlos Smith, Karen Taylor-Good, Jon Vezner and Paul Williams.

To our friends at ASCAP, especially Ralph Murphy; our friends at BMI, especially Perry Howard; Woody Bomar of Sony Music Publishing, Lou Heffernan of American Songwriter Magazine; Karen Taylor-Good; and Thom Schuyler for believing in our project and offering their endorsements.

To our camp at NSAI, which includes David Rivers, National Workshops Director, Mary Beth Stone, N.Y. Regional Workshop Coordinator and Craig Lackey, L.A. Regional Workshop Coordinator, for being the centerpiece of our information gathering.

To Suzanne Thompson, for generously sharing her years of knowledge and experience by giving us a crash course in the world of book printing, saving us God knows how many hours we would have spent learning the hard way (not to mention the expense!).

To Wendy Sager Pomerantz, Jim McCormick, Corley Roberts and Pam Simmons for making us look good with their proofreading expertise.

To Mike Simmons, who deserves sainthood for coming to our rescue when Gracie's computer went on the blink (twice!); Sherrill Blackman, for his insight; and Richard Helm, for letting us include his wonderful lyrics.

To Mark Johnson of Gecko Graphics, for his amazing graphic art skills and overseeing our project when we were plumb worn out at the end, and Artis Betts at Express Media for giving these first-time authors so much attention.

To Gabriel Asher Hollombe, for being Gracie's son and for designing our beautiful website. (Note to Gabe from Gracie: Keep writing. You make me proud!)

A DEEP, HEARTFELT THANK YOU TO YOU ALL.

See you on the charts!

Jerry & Gracie,
Proud Authors

About the use of gender in this workbook:

Sometimes we wrote "he". Sometimes we wrote "she". Sometimes we wrote "his" and sometimes we wrote "hers". Sometimes we wrote "he/she", "his/hers" and "their or theirs". We wrote whatever felt right at the time. We're not sexists, chauvinists or feminists, so please don't be offended. If it's grammatically incorrect, we're kind of sorry. We just did it. Blame it on our parents.

INTRODUCTION

Your first cut.

By definition, it's the first time someone records your song. It's that simple. But a simple definition can't do your first cut justice. It means so much more.

You're a dreamer. A songwriter. You see life a little differently. You hear a story in a heartbreak, a lyric in a conversation, a melody in a sunrise. You have a dream that someone else will hear it like you do.

Your first cut. There's someone out there who sings, performs and touches people's lives with their music. And now for the first time, they want _your_ song to become _their_ song.

Think about it. An artist is willing to put their career on the line to perform your creation, your baby. It means you actually might be able to play in the big leagues of the music business. It means you are going to see your name in teeny-tiny print in parentheses under the title. It means you actually might make some money on your song (don't get your hopes up here).

But what it really means is someone, somewhere out there in the heartland is going to hear your music, your words and your thoughts. You may never meet them, but you do connect on a level that supersedes any other type of communication. And that connection will continue long after you leave this planet.

Your first cut. When you get it, everything makes sense. The rejection, the frustration and the bruised sense of self-esteem gets temporarily forgotten. It even sometimes feels like it was worth it. It even (shudder this thought) felt necessary. One thing is for sure, it makes it all taste a lot sweeter.

Your first cut. We know how much you want it. We know how you can taste it. How it feels out of reach, maybe even insurmountable. It isn't. It takes an incredible amount of discipline and determination, but it can be a reality.

This book is about goals. Little ones. We know your big one. We want you to focus on the little ones and not worry about the big one. The little ones will get you to the big one. We've got a lot of little ones for you, and we want you to take them one step at a time.

The best place to start is always at the beginning. This book is no exception. Take your time and let's put this thing together - together.

Your first cut. Now let's go get it.

HOW TO USE THIS BOOK

There are an almost uncountable number of "How-To" books that deal with songwriting and the music business: how to write lyrics, how to write melodies, how to demo songs, how to network, how to craft song structure, how to market your music, ad infinitum. We know. They are lining our own bookshelves. They are informative and easy to read. They are also easy to put down. Too easy.

This is not a "How To" book. It's a "Do It" book. A behaviorally-centered, goal-oriented workbook designed to make you get your hands dirty and be a human <u>DO</u>ing when it comes to your songs. Although the lofty goal of getting your first cut is the final aspiration here, you'll find it is like a steep staircase on a pyramid leading to that cut. Each step is its own goal in itself. It's been our labor of love to break down those steps for you and set up activities, exercises and approaches to getting you on that first step and from there, up onto the next, and then the next, and the next.

Through our own experiences, and those of other successful songwriters we have come to know and observe, we have seen many diverse staircases for everyone. In fact, each writer's success story is a unique one, but we've also noticed several common denominators that were the major factors in their successes. It's these common denominators <u>we</u> have focused on for <u>you</u> to focus on.

If you feel stuck, if you feel like there's a brick wall you can't get around, if you feel lost, if you feel overwhelmed by what to do next, this workbook is for you. If you feel lazy, if you feel like everyone else is to blame for your songs not getting recognized, if you feel like the world owes you songwriting success while you sit back strumming a G chord, put this book down and go to a movie.

Still with us? Good.

Think of this process then as climbing a pyramid. A songwriting pyramid, if you will. The pyramid looks something like this:

<u>Your First Cut!</u>

<u>Chapters 16, 17, 18, 19, 20</u>

<u>Chapters   14,   15</u>

<u>Chapters   10,   11,   12,   13</u>

<u>Chapters   6,   7,   8,   9</u>

<u>Chapters   1,   2,   3,   4,   5</u>

Each level is a foundation for the next. It's a long climb on this pyramid. Your only desire is to reach the top, but you can't get there in one giant step. You have to take it one at a time. You'll be tempted to skip a few of those steps and jump ahead to get closer to the top. We urge you not to, *even when it seems obvious* that you can.

This is a goal-setting, goal-accomplishing workbook designed so that achieving one goal sets you up to achieve the next. That's why it's important to start at the beginning and then move on to the next one and then the next. Some of the steps are very easy and will take you only a short amount of time to reach. Others might seem almost impossible and take a long time, a great deal of work, planning and dedication. However, *it's important to understand that each step is a valuable one and will make the next one easier.* So don't skip. The top of that pyramid can stay in your sights, but keep your eye on the step you just set your foot on.

Start first with the questionnaire. That's why it's in the front of this workbook. Take it in pencil. If you stick with this program, you'll find you will eventually be adding more points to your answers as you go. Pencil erasers aren't only for correcting mistakes. In this book they are there to show you that you're making progress too. As you accomplish a goal, go back to the questionnaire and adjust your point value, then raise your total. Wear that thing out.

Once you've completed the questionnaire and found where you fit in to how close you are to getting your first cut, look it over. See where your weaknesses are, but also note your strengths. Those strengths are important to remember. They will help you keep going when you feel a little discouraged and give you an even bigger boost when you're jumping over another hurdle.

Each question has a companion chapter that first discusses why this question is an important step to getting your first cut. Read that discussion so you get its importance, and make it a part of your information database in that left-brain hemisphere of yours.

After the discussion is a little commitment statement for you to read and sign. The commitment statement looks something like this:

✏️➤ COMMITMENT:
In order to move closer to getting my first cut,
I will do at least one thing each day, no matter how large or small,
to further my songwriting career.

_____________________________   _______________________________________

         Date   Signed

Make a contract with us and with yourself by signing and dating the commitment statements as you climb the pyramid.

After the commitment statement is a series of exercises designated by a CD symbol that looks like this:

Picture that CD with your first cut on it. Pretty clever, huh? We thought you'd like that. The exercises are designed for you to actively participate in and then when you are finished, to own that question. Each one goes from being a little barrier, to a goal, to an accomplishment. That's what we want you to do. Accomplish the goal of that question. Now, just because you've breezed through answering a question on the questionnaire doesn't mean you can skip that step and not read the discussion. Each step has suggestions to enhance your strengths as well as eliminate your weaknesses. Go through it. Then go to the next.

Now, listen. Now. This is important. ***<u>Do not just read the exercises!</u>*** They are no good to you if you just look at them, yawn, say "OK, I get this one," and then you go watch Monday Night Football, thinking you've accomplished that goal. You haven't. Fill in the lists, the blanks and the check boxes that truly say you have finished that task. Make yourself accountable to yourself. You will not only be surprised at how your level of concentration and commitment changes for the better, but you'll also have reason to be proud of your accomplishments.

Once you've done all the exercises, and you feel you can **<u>honestly</u>** add points to that question, get out that pencil and eraser and go back and fill in the points on the questionnaire. Wear it out some more. Nothing would make us happier than to meet you at some future songwriting workshop and have you showing us your workbook ragged, tattered and worn to a frazzle. At that time we'll be asking you to sing us your song that just got recorded.

The key word to the above paragraph is "honestly". You can do every exercise in the chapter on signing a single-song contract, but until you sign that contract, it's not a done deal. So doing every exercise doesn't necessarily mean you can give yourself those points.

After the exercises, we have added some personal experiences pertaining to that chapter, as well as interviews with hit songwriters and their first cut experiences, that we hope you will enjoy. No testing here. After that, there's a blank page or two (just like when you start a song) headed as "Notes". This is for you to scribble thoughts, ideas, numbers – whatever comes to mind.

Most of all, have fun doing this! We can both attest to the fact that the chase is more fun than holding the brass ring. Keeping the brass ring is another thing altogether and we don't think there's a workbook that can do that. If there is, we'll be using it.

A couple of other things worth mentioning:

First, it may be tempting to do this with a friend. It might be a better idea to have your friend get a book (that way we sell an extra one!) and the two of you get together once a month for added support and to report in on how things are going. While taking group guitar classes, co-writing a cool song, or sneaking into a SESAC #1 party together is all fine, eventually there comes a time when you have to dance alone.

Secondly, we'd like to hear how it's going for you. Log onto our website at www.yourfirstcut.com and click on "Discussion Forum". Go to the bulletin board section with your success stories to encourage others and talk about some of your frustrations as well. Answer some posts with your own advice. We'll be watching, we assure you.

Finally, always remember - <u>always</u> - *your success comes down to writing a great song.* We honestly don't know how to teach you how to do that, and neither does anyone else. But there are plenty of things *you* can do via workshops, song camps, etc. that give you thought provoking information. However only you (and occasionally along with your awesome co-writer) can write a great song. <u>And you have to be doing that all the while you are doing this workbook.</u>

Work hard, stay focused, and good luck!

Gracie and Jerry

HOW CLOSE ARE YOU
TO GETTING YOUR FIRST CUT?

(A Questionnaire)

HOW CLOSE ARE YOU TO GETTING YOUR FIRST CUT?
(A Questionnaire)

1. You play guitar or piano. ____(2 pts)

2. You set aside at least a three-hour block once a week to write. ____(3 pts)

3. You also set aside at least a three-hour block once a week to co-write. ____(3 pts)

4. You are involved in a local songwriting organization (not just a dues-paying member). ____(3 pts)

5. You do at least one thing each day, no matter how large or small, to further your songwriting career. ____(5 pts)

6. You visit a major music center (Nashville, New York or Los Angeles) to attend and play writer's nights, co-write, and network at least three times a year. ____(4 pts)

7. You actively drop off CDs or tapes of your songs to a music center publisher who has agreed to listen to them. ____(4 pts)

8. You have pitched your songs in person to a music center publisher. ____(4 pts)

9. You perform your songs, either solo or in a group or band, in a major music center at least once every two months. ____(3 pts)

10. You live and frequently participate in music industry events within 100 miles of a major music center. ____(10 pts)

11. You co-write on a regular basis with someone who has signed a single-song contract. ____(4 pts)

12. You have signed a single-song contract with a music center publisher. (Add 5 points for every additional contract with a _different_ publisher, but not more than 15 more points. Total possible = 20 pts). ____(5 – 20 pts)

13. You co-write on a regular basis with a writer who has an exclusive songwriting agreement with a music center publisher. ____(5 pts)

14. You have signed an exclusive songwriting agreement with a music center publisher that involves an advance and a demo budget. ____(15 pts)

15. You co-write with a major label recording artist. ____(8 pts)

Total points earned on page one ____

- - continued

16. A publisher has dropped off your song to a major label A&R representative,
    producer or manager.   ____(5 pts)

17. A publisher has played your song to a major label A&R representative,
    a producer's <u>assistant</u> or the manager of a major label recording artist.   ____(7 pts)

18. A publisher has played your song to a producer of a major label recording artist.   ____(9 pts)

19. An A&R rep, artist manager, or a producer has played your song to a major label
    recording artist.   ____(11 pts)

20. A publisher has played your song to a major label recording artist.   ____(12 pts)

Total points earned on this page: ____
Total points earned on previous page: ____
Your score: ____

<u>Your score</u>:

0 - 20:   Now don't be discouraged. Not everyone starts at the top. All hope is not lost. Look at it this way: there's lots of opportunity for improvement. You need to discipline yourself to write and pitch your songs. No excuses, just hunker down and get to work.

21-44:   You do have a steep climb ahead of you, but there's still hope. We know there doesn't seem to be a light in the tunnel yet, but you <u>have</u> begun to build the foundation for your songwriting success. Take a hard look at the answers in which you could not give yourself a score and begin working toward making those goals happen.

45-64:   You are moving in the right direction but it's still not enough. Get out there and exert yourself. Expand your writing and co-writing experiences. Do some networking with other writers and people in the business.

65-84:   You are on the cusp of seriously making it happen.   This is a critical junction for you. Honestly examine your songs and find ways to improve your writing and enhance and expand your business relationships.

85-104:   This is the place where persistence, determination and your ability to take rejection and move on needs to kick in. Continue to take an attitude that there is always room for growth and improvement. Don't give up now.

105-130:   It's just a matter of time here coupled with a lot of luck and a great song. Keep at it. Keep writing.

CHAPTER
1

YOU PLAY GUITAR OR PIANO

YOU PLAY GUITAR OR PIANO

A song consists of two things, lyric and melody. And while there are successful lyrics-only writers, learning an instrument will enhance your creativity regarding melody, rhythm, groove and meter, timing, delivery, dynamics and chord progressions. It's like learning a second language that will make your first language – songwriting – even better.

You don't have to be a master of the instrument. You just have to be willing to learn and be comfortable with it. Make it your friend. Hopefully, you'll be together a long time. Also, learning how to play someone else's song that you regard as special will enhance your appreciation of *that* song and will give you an idea of how to melodically make *your* songs better.

If you write lyrics only, you sometimes fall into a trap of similar meter, melody and rhythm (translation: boring). Playing an instrument will help you get out of some of those traps.

If you already play an instrument, you're not off the hook yet. Sign the commitment statement and move forward to the exercises on page 9. Do not pass go. Do not collect a royalty check.

✏️ COMMITMENT:

*In order to move closer to getting my first cut, as a songwriter desiring to
expand my abilities in melody and meter, I will learn how to play guitar or piano
and/or improve my playing abilities.*

___________________________   ____

Date   Signed

If you don't own a guitar or keyboard, you have at least three choices: buy, borrow or rent. We'll go in that order.

Begin your quest by finding a friend who's knowledgeable on the instrument of your choice and ask him/her to accompany you to pawn shops, used instrument stores and garage sales advertising musical instruments. You don't have to buy it today. Make it an adventure, with your friend playing the instruments and explaining to you the positives and negatives of the instrument at hand. You're in the research phase. It's like buying a new car -- take test drives before buying. Be realistic with your budget. It's not necessary to spend $795 on a new instrument that you haven't learned to play yet. There are many inexpensive instruments that are great to learn on.

 ## RESEARCHING INSTRUMENTS

List below 5 places you visited and priced the musical instrument of your choice. Note the name
of the store you visited, the brand and model of the instrument, its price, and any comments you
have about what you and/or your friend like or dislike about the instrument.

Store	Brand and Model	Price	Personal Comments

BORROWING AN INSTRUMENT

Instead of buying, if you have a friend who owns an entry-level guitar or keyboard that they're
not using, offer 10% of your first royalty check to borrow it for a month (first royalty checks
are usually less than $8, but we won't tell). Ask him to show you how to play a D chord, an A
chord and how to play "Tom Dooley". Once your fingers stop hurting and you've become bored (and
feel like you need therapy from hanging from a wide oak tree this time tomorrow), you can give
yourself permission to buy.

Write your friend's name below and the make and model of the instrument they're loaning to you:

Friend's Name: _________________________   Instrument: _________________________

RENTING AN INSTRUMENT

If you don't have any friends, rent an instrument from your local music store. Let your fingers do
the walking and call 5 music stores. Research their rental rates for your instrument:

Music Store	Phone Number	Instrument	Rental Prices

Note: Just calling the above won't get you points for this chapter. Remember the key word is
<u>PLAY</u>. Once you get your instrument you need to learn how to play it.

If you already own an instrument or if you just got one as a result of the preceding activities, continue below.

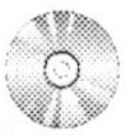 GROUP OR PRIVATE LESSONS

Find a place to take lessons. Several cities have free classes offered as community services in local universities. There also may be community centers (public and private) offering low-cost classes. Group classes are a great way to start.

List 3 places, their phone numbers and the cost of their lessons below. Note if the lessons are group or private:

Store/Organization   Phone Number   Cost of Lessons   Group/Private

____

____

____

Now sign up and take some lessons. Don't quit. Remember, the key word is PLAY.

 EDUCATIONAL RESOURCES

Search the Internet by typing "guitar lessons" into your favorite search engine. We went on "Ask Jeeves" and found dozens of sites offering everything from learning on the 'net to ordering specialty videos for all levels and musical tastes. If you are a loner (and what songwriter isn't at times?) or living in a shack in the Montana back country, this could be a good way for you to go.

List 3 websites offering online lessons on the instrument of your choice:
1. www.___________________________________.com
2. www.___________________________________.com
3. www.___________________________________.com

List 3 websites offering opportunities to purchase books, videos or lessons on CD for the instrument of your choice:

                    Website   Product   Price
1. www._______________________________.com ____________________ _________
2. www._______________________________.com ____________________ _________
3. www._______________________________.com ____________________ _________

 ## IMPROVING YOUR TECHNIQUE

If you already have some knowledge of an instrument and would like to improve, you can use this opportunity to find out about private teachers in your area.

List 3 teachers or organizations that offer intermediate or advanced group lessons and their phone numbers:

Teacher/Organization   Phone Number and Rate

____

____

____

Now sign up and take some lessons. Don't quit. Remember again, the key word is PLAY.

 ## MASTERING YOUR PERFORMANCE SKILLS

Practice. Get better. Learn 3 of your favorite songs until you can play them without making a mistake. List them below and the date on which you are able to play each one flawlessly:

Song Title   Date of Mastery

____

____

____

After you have completed the above, learn 3 more, then 3 after that.

As you begin learning your instrument, be patient with yourself and have fun. Remember that this process is intended to improve your songwriting skills and to give you a better insight of melody, rhythm and meter. You'll find that as you continue to practice and improve, so will your songwriting.

Don't go down to join the Musician's Union just yet thinking you're ready to audition for the Paul Schaffer Band. But don't rule it out either.

JV:

My first guitar was a "Lindell". I bought it for $27.50. After hearing someone play "500 Miles" at a church camp, I took a bus to a downtown Kansas City pawnshop, paid cash (15 year-olds didn't have checking accounts in those days), then walked two blocks away to a music store and bought a Mel Bay Method guitar book. I eventually gave my Lindell to my high school sweetheart. She married a U.S. Congressman. I don't miss her, but I sure miss my first guitar.

GH:

My first guitar was made of plywood. Its top had a yellow stain (it couldn't pass for spruce if it tried!). I had begged for a guitar and my mom didn't want to invest a lot of money if I was (in her words) "going to quit in two weeks". I think it cost $35. I was 12 and she signed me up for group classes. When I was 17, I got a summer job at a guitar shop and saved every penny to buy a new guitar for $135. I still own it.

* * * * *

From Paul Williams

"I had my first two recordings released the same day. Claudine Longet released an album on A&M Records with the song `It's Hard to Say Goodbye'. That same day, Tiny Tim's recording of `Tiptoe thru the Tulips' was released with a song called `Fill Your Heart' on the B-side.  It's a song that I wrote with the very talented Biff Rose, and we were thrilled when, years later, David Bowie included it on his `Hunky Dorey' album. It was the first outside song he ever recorded.

"A few months after a publisher told me I 'didn't have a future in music', Biff went in to meet with Chuck Kaye at A&M's publishing wing, and their meeting led to both of us being signed as writers. Thank you, Biff."

- Paul Williams
ASCAP, Grammy, Golden Globe and Oscar award-winning songwriter with songs recorded by artists ranging from Barbara Streisand to Diamond Rio. Paul was inducted into the Songwriters Hall Of Fame in 2001.

* * * * *

<u>Paul's advice to songwriters</u>:
"Write authentic `You'. Don't try to be anybody else. Put what touches you into your songs and you'll probably touch everyone else. We're pretty much alike as people, and your emotional honesty is powerful. Also, have a life and learn to play golf if you don't know how. It'll be a big part of your sanity when the great ones don't get cut.

"The talent that's pounding in your chest isn't a punishment. It's a gift that you're supposed to share. God wants you to be heard."

NOTES

NOTES

CHAPTER
2

YOU SET ASIDE AT LEAST A THREE-HOUR BLOCK ONCE A WEEK TO WRITE

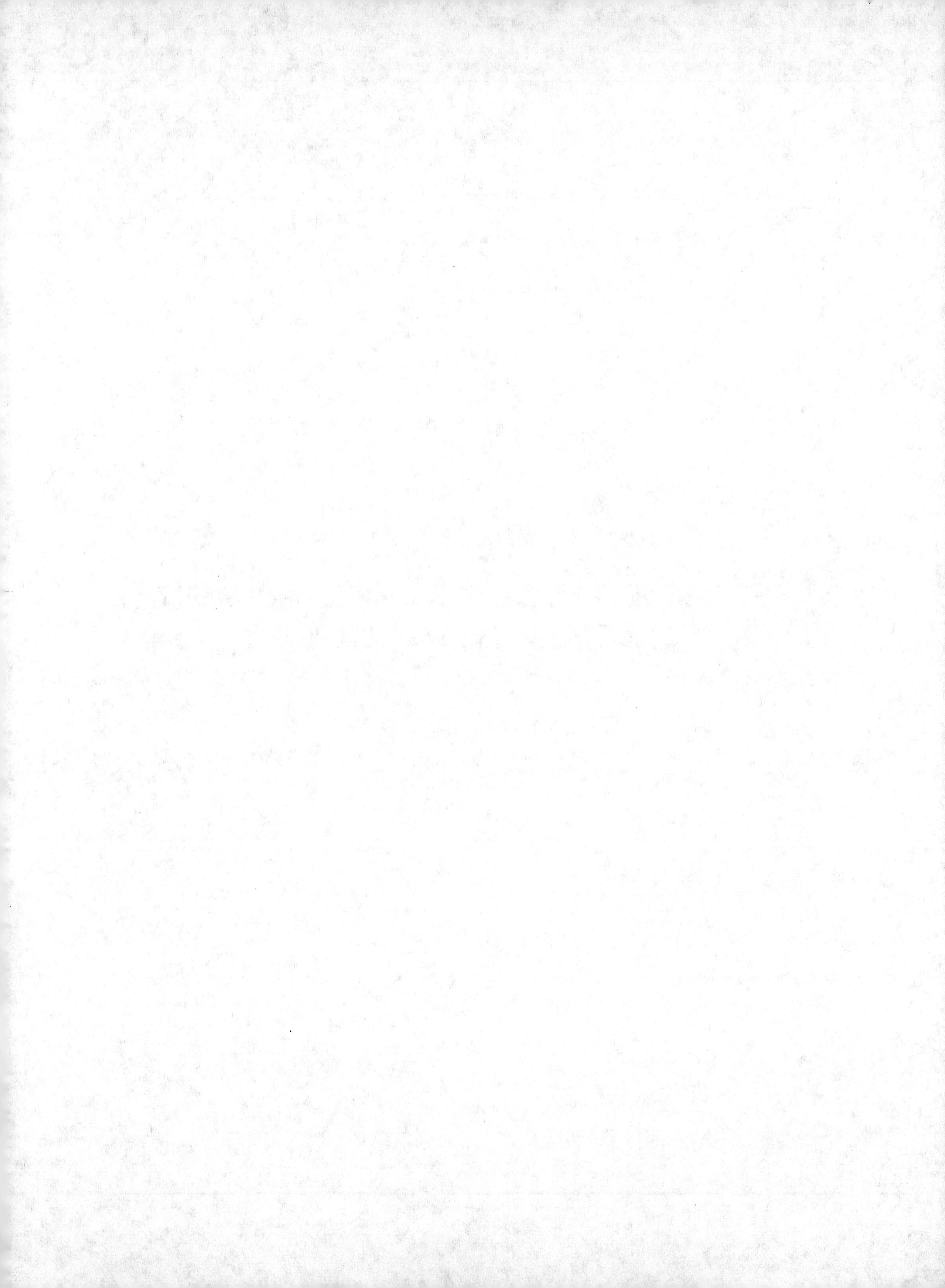

YOU SET ASIDE AT LEAST A THREE-HOUR BLOCK
ONCE A WEEK TO WRITE

There's an old adage, "The harder I work, the luckier I get". You won't get better at songwriting if you don't write. Productivity eventually equals quality. The more you write, the better your songs will be. Setting aside a disciplined time in your life demonstrates to you and the world around you that this is your passion and you're serious about it. Besides, you want to build a catalog for the music business to hear. Won't it be nice when that producer says, "I like this song. What else do you have?", and you can reach in your pocket and show him?

Why a three-hour block? One hour is just enough time to change your mind and go wash the dishes. Two hours is just enough time to come up with an idea and blame that blank piece of paper for not giving you more. Three hours is just enough time to get the creative juices flowing and to have something to show for it. You don't have to finish a song; you just have to write it. Finishing it will come in your next three-hour block, or maybe the next. Don't worry. If you write it, it will come.

▭▭▭▷ COMMITMENT:

In order to move closer to getting my first cut,
I will, as a disciplined songwriter, set aside at least a three-hour block once a week to write:

_______________________   ______________________________________

Date   Signed

YOUR MOST OPPORTUNE TIME TO WRITE

Research your most opportune time to write. What night does your significant other watch Star Trek reruns? What time do the kids go to bed? What night do your friends <u>not</u> call you to go out? Is the weekend the best time? Don't put yourself in a time slot that will eventually be compromised. Tell others in your household that this time by yourself is important to you and ask them to honor that. Give them the opportunity to support you by not making demands that would distract you from your goal.

List 5 possible days and times of the week that are most convenient to you and your family for your writing time:

Day of the Week: ______________________________   Time: ______________________________
Day of the Week: ______________________________   Time: ______________________________
Day of the Week: ______________________________   Time: ______________________________
Day of the Week: ______________________________   Time: ______________________________
Day of the Week: ______________________________   Time: ______________________________

 ## MAKING AN APPOINTMENT WITH YOURSELF

Grab your calendar. Pick a day (or evening) this week from your list and make an appointment with yourself.   Then, mark three-hour blocks each week for the next four weeks. Make this commitment to yourself non-negotiable (put it in ink!). It will be easy to come up with excuses to reschedule your appointment. Don't disappoint yourself by keeping that song inside you that's waiting to come out. (Note: If you're afraid of missing the latest installment of Survivor, tape it!)

Note the day and time below of your appointment with yourself (in ink).

Day of the Week: ________________________________   Time: ____________________________

Shortly after you have started the next Grammy award-winning song-of-the-year classic, take your supporters to Dairy Queen for a double hot fudge shake to say "thanks!".

COMPLETING YOUR FIRST "SOLO WRITE"

Get out your guitar or keyboard, a sharp pencil, a writing tablet and turn off the phone. After you have completed your first "solo write", tell us about it. Put the song title below and the date of its creation next to it.

Song Title: ____   Date of Creation: ______________

Good job! Pat yourself on the back and remember to keep your appointment next week. You should find that eventually that blank sheet of paper becomes more of a friend than a foe, and your creative juices will flow more often. This is a great start towards building a catalog of your hit songs. Keep up the good work.

JV:

Before the Slice of Life Restaurant closed in Nashville, I had a routine every Thursday morning: arrive at the Slice at 8:30, order eggs over easy and hash browns and a cup of vanilla nut coffee. After mulling over breakfast and the latest issue of the Nashville Scene (including the personal columns – great song ideas there), I was ready to get to work. I went to my office, locked the door behind me, turned off the phone, got out my guitar, paper and pencil, and wrote. I didn't always come up with gems, but I always came up with something. That routine has built a foundation for me to write 3-6 songs a year by myself and also create partial songs that I could later bring to co-writing sessions. Only one of those songs has ever been cut, and that cut never even paid for the demo. It's one that I'm not only proud to say I wrote, but it's a testimonial to the discipline process. Even though "The Slice" closed, I will always remember it fondly for its part in getting me ready every Thursday for my creative day.

GH:

I remember how hard it used to be to allow time for "me" in my schedule. I was a single mom, and my energy was needed in a lot of different areas, most of them having nothing to do with fulfilling my creative needs. It was easier to drive my son to and from school, pack his lunch, drive him to his friend's house, help him with his homework, etc., than it was to set aside a few hours for me and my needs. When I did, I always would feel so guilty -- until one day I realized that 100 years from now no one will know if my house was spotless or not, or if I did the dishes that night right after eating dinner. In order to make a positive change in my habits, I began giving myself gold stars on my calendar every time I kept my commitment to myself. Then I trained myself to focus on the stars and not the spaces in between.

* * * * *

From Pat Alger

"My first major cut was 'First Time Love' by singer/songwriter Livingston Taylor. In 1980 it was on an album titled 'Man's Best Friend' and was released as a single going to #38 on the Billboard pop chart and #13 on the AC charts. I was making my living as a singer/songwriter in a duo with Artie Traum, and we had the opportunity to open a show for Livingston. Backstage, he was listening to us warm up, and he asked for a tape of some of my songs. The next week I sent him a boom box demo on cassette of three songs, two of which he ended up cutting, and both were hit singles. The second one, 'City Lights' was a duet with his brother James and went to # 17 on The Billboard AC charts. For a couple of years they performed it as a duet in James' shows. I had been living in Manhattan and was considering moving back to my native Georgia when, in the Spring of 1980, I made an exploratory drive to Atlanta to check out the music scene there. On that drive, somewhere in North Carolina (Livingston's home state), I picked up a weak signal going through the mountains and caught the last verse and chorus. I was all alone and almost drove off the mountain trying to tune that station in."

-Pat Alger
ASCAP award-winning songwriter with over 100 songs recorded, including those by Dolly Parton, Kathy Mattea, Trisha Yearwood, Hal Ketchum, and four number ones for Garth Brooks, including "Unanswered Prayers" and "The Thunder Rolls"

* * * * *

<u>Pat's advice to songwriters:</u>
"Listen to everyone's advice and don't take any of it too personally. When you find everyone saying about the same thing concerning your work, it might be time to take some of it to heart, good or bad. In the end, to have a long career that is going to be satisfying, you must always write what comes naturally in your own voice."

NOTES

NOTES

CHAPTER
3

YOU ALSO SET ASIDE AT LEAST A THREE-HOUR BLOCK ONCE A WEEK TO CO-WRITE

YOU ALSO SET ASIDE AT LEAST A THREE-HOUR BLOCK
ONCE A WEEK TO CO-WRITE

Co-writing is a special way to give and receive ideas regarding lyric, melody, meter, song development, and every other creative aspect that enters into your next masterpiece. You may have a song idea called "Angels Can Fly" and think that the storyline of the song would be about your loved one being so perfect that she should be able to fly. Not a bad idea (probably a ballad), but is there a better one? Your co-writer might have a completely different "take" on it, such as angels can fly because they take themselves lightly -- obviously an idea that may create an entirely new approach to melody and lyrics (fun & up-tempo) -- thus the distinct advantage to co-writing. Two (or more) writers working together can brainstorm an unlimited number of ideas and approaches to a song that neither writer would have come up with by themselves.

Co-writing also helps you maintain your discipline. It's harder to walk away from that line you are stuck on when you are in a partnership that has the common goal of finishing a great song. It isn't so easy to cancel that writing appointment when someone else is expecting you to be there. A trusting co-writer won't let you get by with that mediocre line in the second verse or that predictable five-chord setting up the chorus. (One of my co-writers tells me I'm "pegging her gag meter" – JV.) Co-writing also instills a responsibility to "come to the table" with ideas and an intention to be in a creative state of mind.

Co-writing is a teacher and a student. You both have things to offer to the other in a unique setting. You know that cool guitar lick she came up with as a signature to the song? Now you have to learn it, and that makes you a better guitar player next time you write. That twisted little way you talk about how you ended up in the BFI relationship dumpster last Valentine's Day inspires her to see lyrical approaches in a way she never thought of before. The sky is the limit, and it's easier to reach for it with your co-writer.

Best of all, you share a special friendship with someone in the creation of something that never existed before, and no amount of awards, royalty checks or #1 parties will ever equal that. If you co-write you will become a better writer, and becoming a better writer will bring you closer to your first cut.

Now let's get you ready to co-write.

COMMITMENT:
In order to move closer to getting my first cut,
I will set aside a three-hour block at least once a week to co-write.

_______________________   _______________________
            Date   Signed

Finding a co-writer isn't much different than dating. You do need to be somewhat selective. After all, if you wouldn't go out with that guy that still lives with his mother and gets his kicks out of watching the girls on the front row of the WWF on Saturday nights, you probably wouldn't want to share those intimate song ideas with him either.

 ASSESSING YOUR STRENGTHS

Consider your songwriting strengths. Now consider your songwriting weaknesses. (We know you don't have any, but humor us here). Are you a master at soaring ballad melodies but clueless to how a good R&B groove works?   Do you express yourself with words and images that would make Dickens look like an amateur but need twenty lines to get to the first chorus? List your strengths on the left side and what you wish your co-writers' strengths to be on the right.

MY STRENGTHS: CO-WRITER STRENGTHS WISH LIST:

_______________________   _______________________
_______________________   _______________________
_______________________   _______________________
_______________________   _______________________
_______________________   _______________________

Now you have a starting place for your co-writer search.

There are an infinite number of places to go on your co-writer search. The local songwriter's organization that meets every second Tuesday of the month is a good place to start. The bulletin board in your nearby music store might at this very moment have a posting from a writer looking for you. The coffee house downtown (you know, the one with the brick wall behind the stage) is featuring a local up-and-coming songwriter this very weekend who would love to look at your lyrics. There's a bookstore with a café upstairs that features local artists just beginning to write and at this very moment are also reading this workbook. The junior college that inserts a flyer every quarter about their evening writing classes is teeming with potential co-writers. The Thirsty Tadpole has just started a Monday night open mic with a ton of co-writers performing and commiserating. Check it out. Check it all out.

 ## CO-WRITER SEARCH

List 5 places, venues or institutions for you to go to check out potential co-writers. Go there.
After visiting each, write down the place and the date that you went.

<u>Name</u>   <u>Date Visited</u>

____

____

____

____

____

Approaching a co-writer is very scary, but you are going to have to put aside those latent fears you have about rejection (this goes with the entire music business territory – get used to it). There are ways to ease into this, however. Let him or her know how much you admire his or her songs, especially the melodies. Add that you'd like to offer a sample of some of your songs with the idea of maybe getting together sometime and trying to crank out a hit. As a matter of fact, you happen to have a lyric that needs a cool melody a lot like the groove on that second to the last song of theirs. Would he or she like to look at it sometime? Maybe they will, but then again maybe they won't. This is just like dating, remember? Be friendly and polite. Eventually, you'll find a match.

POTENTIAL CO-WRITERS

Now list five potential co-writers you met, along with their phone numbers and email addresses:

<u>Name</u>   <u>Phone Number</u>   <u>Email Address</u>

____

____

____

____

____

 ## CALLING A NEW CO-WRITER AND MAKING AN APPOINTMENT

Pick a name from the previous list, make a call and make an appointment. After you do so, fill in the chart below.

Name: ____

Phone #: ________________________________   Email Address: _____________________________

Date Called: _____________________________   Appointment Date: __________________________

Place: ____

Arrive on time with a positive, upbeat attitude, a goal to getting a song started, and some great ideas that you are excited about. (Translation: be prepared.)

CO-WRITING PROGRESS

After you have completed your co-write, tell us about it. Put the song title below and the date of creation next to it.

Song Title: ______________________________________   Date of Creation: ______________

Writers' Names: ____

We can see it all the way from here. Your self-discipline (and your co-writer's) is paying off. Now make a new appointment. Keep it up. You're getting closer.

JV: I could go on forever about my co-writing experiences. I've met co-writers in clubs, restaurants, restrooms and even in a potential copyright infringement lawsuit! In addition to the standard Nashville meeting places (office and home), I've had writing appointments in fast food restaurants, on picnic tables and even in a canoe in the Canadian wilderness.

Once I had written a song by myself about getting over a recent heartbreak. It was syrupy, new age, poetic, and bland. (I didn't know that at the time.) I played it for one of my co-writers at our regular Monday morning session and, after recognizing a cool idea, she suggested several lyric and melody changes. I enthusiastically agreed, and a few sessions later we finished a song called "Don't Waste It On The Blues", which went on to not only be my first cut, but a #5 ASCAP award-winning song in 1990 and the vehicle for a great writing deal with Little Big Town Music. Are co-writers great, or what?

GH: I was working in a law office (and taking a songwriting class on Saturday mornings) when I discovered that a co-worker of mine wrote screenplays in his spare time. I mentioned to him that I wrote songs and asked if he ever thought of writing songs since, after all, songs are like three-minute movies. He admitted that he had always wanted to write a song, and we decided to get together that next Monday night. It was such a good match that we continued to meet every Monday night for over a year. The best part was the first hour or so when we would catch each other up on our lives.

* * * * *

I'M NOT MAKING ANY MONEY
by Richard Helm

With an idea in our head, a pad of paper on the table
With old guitars resting on our knees
We talk about direction, sometimes we sit in silence
Strum some chords and hum a melody

A song is slowly born and a bond between us grows
As we labor over every word
We struggle to get it right night after night
Hopin' someday our song will be heard

We write and write and write
Then we write it all over again
I'm not making any money
But I'm makin' some real good friends

In between the lines we talk about our lives
We cover all the lows and the highs
We laugh about our funky cars, cry about our broken hearts
Help each other out when money's tight

When our song is finally done and it all comes down to fate
We pack up our guitars and say goodnight
And it always occurs to me as I drive off down the street
These friends are the songs of my life

We write and write and write
Then we write it all over again
I'm not making any money
But I'm makin' some real good friends

© 1985 Richard Helm
Used By Permission

* * * * *

NOTES

NOTES

CHAPTER
4

YOU ARE INVOLVED IN A LOCAL
SONGWRITING ORGANIZATION

YOU ARE INVOLVED IN A
LOCAL SONGWRITING ORGANIZATION

In addition to misery, creativity loves company, and a songwriting association in your area is a great place to connect on everything about your passion for songs and songwriting. Besides, it's not as lonely when you know there is a group out there that you can look forward to meeting with on a regular basis to share ideas, contacts and inspirations. Gracie always describes her feeling after going to her first NSAI workshop in L.A. as "finding her tribe".

These "tribes" offer an abundance of educational resources, networking information, feedback, contacts and, most of all, encouragement. Some of the better organizations have contests, sponsor local performances, set up seminars with music professionals and provide other creative ways for you to make a connection, which leads to writing a better song, which leads to what else? Your first cut!

The key word is "involved". Just going and sitting in the back row won't get the job done. You need to be active in presenting and listening to others' songs, offering your constructive feedback, your experiences in acceptance and rejection, and your charming personality to keep the meeting upbeat and informative. You only get out of it what you put into it.

Maybe you have some great organizational skills that will help your local group set up a contest, seminar or guest speaker. Maybe you are a good administrator who can organize meetings, times and places. Whatever your strengths, don't be afraid to get your hands dirty. Dig in.

By the way, co-writers are coming out of the woodwork here. They might be looking for you!

COMMITMENT:
In order to move closer to getting my first cut
I will become an active, involved member in my local songwriting organization.

_______________________   _______________________
Date   Signed

There are many associations in the United States at your service. Let's begin with the two national organizations. The first is:

The Nashville Songwriters Association International (NSAI)
1701 West End Avenue, 3rd Floor
Nashville, TN 37203
(615) 256-3354
1-800-321-6008
Website address: www.nashvillesongwriters.com

NSAI has more than 100 "regional workshops" not only in the U.S., but also in Canada, Europe and even in New Zealand. There is probably one near you. The workshop mission is to "educate and elevate" the songwriter. To that end they teach the craft *and* business of songwriting.

The other national songwriter's organization is the Songwriters Guild of America. The Guild actually has three offices, all in major music centers:

<u>Los Angeles office</u>	<u>Nashville office</u>	<u>New York office</u>
6430 Sunset Blvd., #705	1222 16th Ave. South, #25	1560 Broadway, #1306
Hollywood, CA 90028	Nashville, TN 37212	New York, NY 10036
(323) 462-5430	(615) 329-1782	(212) 768-7902

All three offices share the same website at www.songwriters.org. They also offer many incredibly valuable workshops, "Ask-a-Pro" Q&A sessions, and critique meetings. Each office also offers events unique to their area, such as "rewrite workshops" in L.A., "Songmania" in Nashville, and "Pro-Shop" in New York. There are even some Q&A and critique opportunities online. The SGA folks are great people. Even if you don't live in one of the above cities, you owe it to yourself to check them out.

There are also many independent groups all over that offer terrific opportunities for networking and education. One of three websites -- www.musesmuse.com, www.songwriteruniverse.com or Just Plain Folks at www.jpfolks.com -- should be able to lead you to an organization near you. See the list of resources in the appendix of this workbook.

At the time of this printing, the only national songwriter's organization that sponsors groups outside of the major music centers is NSAI, so let's look there first.

 ## RESEARCHING NSAI

Contact NSAI and ask if there's a local regional workshop near you. If there is no workshop within an hour's drive from you, go to the exercise, "Local Songwriting Group Info" on page 38, and start there. If there is a local workshop, ask for the coordinators' names, phone numbers and email. Write them down here:

Chapter Name:　　　　　____
Coordinator(s) Name(s):　________________________　________________________
Phone Number(s):　　　__________________________　________________________
Email:　　　　　　　　__________________________　________________________

LOCAL NSAI WORKSHOP INFO

Good. Now call the coordinator and write down the date, time and place of their next meeting here:

Date:　　　____
Time:　　　____
Place:　　　____

Directions to get there:

____
____
____
____

WORKSHOP NOTES

Okay, "Fear Factor" is a re-run this week. Get off the couch and go to that meeting. To prove to us you went, write a brief description of the meeting. How many others were there? What was the agenda of the meeting? Were any songs played? Are there any potential co-writers?

____
____
____
____

WORKSHOP SCHEDULE

Now go back to the next meeting. When is it? _______________________________________

Put it in your calendar in ink.

LOCAL SONGWRITING GROUP INFO

Some cities have more than just NSAI workshops. Some may not have an NSAI group at all, but still have a songwriter's organization that is operating successfully. Go to the internet, the phone book, music stores, etc. and look to see if that's the case for your area. If you find one (or even more than one), write down the contact person's name and phone number here:

Group Name: ____
Contact Name: ____
Phone Number: ____

MORE LOCAL SONGWRITING GROUP INFO

Good. Now call the contact person and write down the date, time and place of their next meeting here:

Date: ____
Time: ____
Place: ____

Directions to get there:

____

____

____

____

LOCAL SONGWRITING GROUP NOTES

Okay, "Friends" is a re-run this week. Get off the couch and go to that meeting. To prove to us you went, write a brief description of the meeting. How many others were there? What was the agenda of the meeting? Were any songs played? Are there any potential co-writers?

____

____

____

____

 ## LOCAL SONGWRITING GROUP SCHEDULE

Now go back to the next meeting. When is it? _______________________________________
Put it in your calendar in ink.

If you are new to the local songwriting organization scene, you are off to a good start in this area. If you are already active in your group, keep it up and don't let down. In either case, do some more research and find if there is another independent association near you. Follow up the same way you did above.

You didn't know there was so much out there, did you? And you thought you were all alone. You're not. But you will be if you don't get involved.

Attend, attend, attend. You can benefit from more than one organization. They all have something to offer. You can't do too much when it comes to getting that first cut. Participate.

JV:
When I finally got serious about songwriting, I found that Kansas City had a local independent songwriters' organization. I joined immediately and went to my first meeting scared to death that everybody would hate my songs. Just the opposite happened. I found encouragement, information, and new friends that kept me serious about forging ahead. When I moved to Nashville, the first doors I walked through were the NSAI office and the Songwriters Guild. I found the same resources there, and what I learned through them contributed directly to the success of obtaining my first cut. As a pro member of NSAI and SGA, I continue to receive those benefits. I sincerely believe I would not have had my songs recorded without those organizations in my corner.

GH:
I may never be able to figure out why it took so long for me to join NSAI. I was on a quest to connect with fellow songwriters when I was living in Los Angeles, and it was after I finally made that connection that I retraced my steps and discovered I had been referred to joining NSAI nine times! Am I glad I joined? You bet.

This is clearly one of those cases where you can learn from my mistakes and not have to make them yourself! So if you're not involved a local songwriting organization yet, what are you waiting for?

---

* * * * *

From Jason Blume

"I once had a tiny independent cut on an artist produced by Don Goodman, so I decided to capitalize on my newfound credibility and scheduled my first trip to Nashville in order to write with Don.

"He never did show up for our writing appointment. His publisher felt terrible about it, so she went down the hall and returned with another writer, A. J. Masters, who she'd convinced to try working with me. We took one of my "starts" and polished it into "Change My Mind", my first major label cut, which was recorded and released as a single by the Oak Ridge Boys in 1991.

"Although the single didn't do well, it got me my first staff writing deal, which led to my songs getting recorded by Britney Spears and the Backstreet Boys, to date totaling over 45 million records."

-Jason Blume
BMI award-winning songwriter with recordings by Collin Raye, Britney Spears, the Backstreet Boys, J'Son (included in "First Kid", a hit Disney film, as well as becoming a #1 video on B.E.T.), Steve Azar, MC Potts, 3 of Hearts, Solid HarmoniE, and Boyz 'N Girlz United. His songs have been performed on TV shows including the "Miss America Pageant", "The Guiding Light", "Fame", and "Dangerous Minds". Jason is also the author of <u>6 Steps to Songwriting Success: The Comprehensive Guide to Writing and Marketing Hit Songs</u>, published by Billboard Books.

* * * * *

<u>Jason's advice to songwriters:</u>
"My advice to developing songwriters is the same thing I tell myself each time I sit down to write. Acquire all of the tools that you can and have them in your proverbial toolbox, but then push the envelope, think outside the box and create something new and original. As I often write when I autograph my books, 'Follow your dreams -- and enjoy the ride.'"

NOTES

NOTES

CHAPTER
5

YOU DO AT LEAST ONE THING EACH DAY, NO MATTER HOW LARGE OR SMALL, TO FURTHER YOUR SONGWRITING CAREER

YOU DO AT LEAST ONE THING EACH DAY, NO MATTER HOW LARGE OR SMALL, TO FURTHER YOUR SONGWRITING CAREER

> *"Everyday when I wake up I think of this business as a board game and I want to move my piece further along."*
> *-Sherrill Blackman, Publisher and Song Plugger*

This may actually be the most important goal for you to accomplish. And it's one that should stay with you throughout your career. It is your way of <u>maintaining focus</u> 7 days a week, 365 days a year. Think of it as a "One-A-Day" vitamin. When you take your vitamin each day, it does what you want it to do. It puts nutrients in your body, makes you a little more resistant to disease and, more importantly, keeps your attention on your good health. When you forget to take your vitamin, not only does your body not receive those benefits, but you are also not focused on your goal.

So it is also with <u>maintaining a discipline</u> to be active in your goal of getting your first cut. You don't have to have a huge monumental goal every day. If your "vitamin" is to call EMI Publishing and demand a publishing deal on the spot, your rejection factor may skyrocket, causing a setback. The wound that will be inflicted on you will be so deep, that you're going to have to take more "One-A-Days" just to stop the bleeding. And that's not the kind of first cut we're talking about! That goal is too big.

We're talking about simple, <u>small</u>, easy approaches to keep your thought processes moving in the right direction. Call a co-writer and make an appointment. Get out a Tim McGraw CD ("Everywhere" is a good choice - Jerry will get 1.2 cents for it), and listen to each song. Think about why Tim would want to cut that song. Go to the library and read the latest issue of Billboard Magazine. Go to a movie to get a song idea. Gather together all the little slips of songwriting ideas scratched on Brown's Diner napkins sitting on your desk, and type them in your computer. Restring your guitar. You get the picture. Small tasks, or as Julia Cameron (author of "The Artist's Way") would say, "small do-able tasks".

Discipline is key here. If you don't take your vitamins, they don't work. If you do, they will. It's that simple. Eventually, you should find yourself maintaining a steady thought process that will inevitably factor in to your becoming a better writer, which will get you that cut.

COMMITMENT:

In order to move closer to getting my first cut,
I will do at least one thing each day, no matter how large or small,
to further my songwriting career.

____________________　　　　____________________
　　　　Date　　　　　　　　　　　　　　　Signed

According to Pavlov, it takes 21 days to form a habit (if, of course, you do it 21 days in a row). Salivating when a bell goes off isn't exactly what we have in mind here, but stay with us for a minute.

 **<u>BRAINSTORM LIST</u>**

List 21 actions you can take (like the examples earlier) toward furthering your songwriting goals that you can refer to later when you can't think of what to do that day. Be creative. They don't have to be in any particular order. Also, don't forget that the key word is "small". You can't do this wrong unless you make the goal too astronomical. Don't spend a lot of time. Brainstorm.

1. _Call Will Robinson and sign up for camp (songwriting)_
2. _record songs already written, 10 or so to get started_
3. _call Dino Bradley and ask him about "I can't be your Mama" song_
4. _call Bambi_
5. _call Dave – guitar if I can't get Right as Rain music_
6. _call John Wiggins, songwriter write in May_
7. _look up number system and learn it_
8. _Nash. Song writers Assoc. belong to it_
9. _ASCAP or (BMI)? submit songs to it_
10. ____
11. ____
12. ____
13. ____
14. ____
15. ____
16. ____
17. ____
18. ____
19. ____
20. ____
21. ____

 ## WEEKLY ACTIONS LIST

Looking at your brainstorm list, plan the actions you'll take for the upcoming week. Then, so that you'll be able to look back and acknowledge your progress, at the end of each day this week, list and record what action you took each day.

Sunday: ____

Monday: ____

Tuesday: ____

Wednesday: ____

Thursday: ____

Friday: ____

Saturday: ____

 ## SUPPORTING YOUR DREAM

Copy the above form and place it where you'll see it every day. Put it on the bathroom mirror, the refrigerator, your computer screen, or the back of your front door. Fill it in each night before you go to sleep and dream of your acceptance speech for your #1 party. Add two points if you also flossed your teeth. (No, no, just kidding).

Every day, really, really, **REALLY** do this. It's too easy not to, but it truly works. You'll be amazed at the results.

Remember that pyramid we talked about in "How To Use This Book?" Congratulations! You just completed level one - - "Your Commitment to Songwriting". Good job. Don't stop now. Keep climbing.

JV:

This is probably my toughest discipline. Sometimes I don't want to think about songwriting. I just want to change the oil in my car. If I took my "vitamins" every day, maybe I'd have a nicer car, and I'd be paying someone else to change my oil. I have definitely found, however, that when I take action, large or small, everyday, even Sundays, I get results. This little system works better than you think. Give it a try.

GH:

I keep a weekly chart on the bulletin board next to my desk at home. The chart has 8 columns. The first column lists things I want to do on a consistent basis such as songwriting, pitching, vocalizing, practicing guitar, etc. (There are also non music-related tasks such as meditation, sit-ups, etc.) Then there are columns for each day of the week. Whenever I complete something on the chart, I draw a star in the box for that day. I only focus on how much I accomplish every week and then pat myself on the back. (If I don't then who will?) It's amazing how far a little positive reinforcement can carry me.

And for extra support, I have one of my favorite quotes at the top of the page. It's by biographer W.H. Murray: "Until one is committed, there is hesitancy, the chance to draw back, always ineffectiveness. Concerning all acts of initiative (and creation), there is one elementary truth – the ignorance of which kills countless ideas and splendid plans: that the moment one definitely commits oneself, then providence moves too. All sorts of things occur to help one that would never otherwise have occurred. A whole stream of events issues from the decision, raising in ones favor all manner of unforeseen incidents and meetings and material assistance, which no person could have dreamed would have come their way."

* * * * *

From Wood Newton

"Actually my first major label recording was on my own album on Elektra/Asylum records in 1979. There were two songs on it that I co-wrote, 'Julie, Do I Ever Cross Your Mind?' and 'Love The Hurt Away.'

"My first 'outside' cut was a song I wrote with Tim Dubois called 'Midnight Hauler.' It was recorded by Razzy Bailey and was also my first single. It went to #1 in 1980. Tim and I had heard about a sci-fi movie entitled 'UFOria' that needed a truck driving song in it, so we sat down and completed 'Midnight Hauler' with that project in mind. The movie never got made, but Razzy's hit allowed me to put a down payment on my first home."

- Wood Newton
BMI award-winning songwriter with a slew of number ones including "Bobby Sue" by the Oak Ridge Boys, "Twenty Years Ago" by Kenny Rogers, "What I Didn't Do" by Steve Wariner and, most recently, "Riding With Private Malone" by David Ball

* * * * *

<u>Wood's advice to songwriters:</u>
"If you do it just for the love of it, a great song will finally rise. Hopefully in your lifetime."

NOTES

CHAPTER
6

YOU VISIT A MAJOR MUSIC CENTER (NASHVILLE, NEW YORK, OR LOS ANGELES) TO ATTEND AND PLAY WRITER'S NIGHTS, CO-WRITE, AND NETWORK AT LEAST THREE TIMES A YEAR

> ## YOU VISIT A MAJOR MUSIC CENTER (NASHVILLE, NEW YORK OR LOS ANGELES) TO ATTEND AND PLAY WRITER'S NIGHTS, CO-WRITE, AND NETWORK AT LEAST 3 TIMES A YEAR

When you enter a contest, there's usually a qualifier at the bottom of the entry form stating "no purchase necessary" and "you need not be present to win". The music business is a different contest. The chances of your songs being heard in your hometown by someone who is closely tied with the powers of the music industry and can make it happen for your song are on the same level as that proverbial "snowball in hell". As a matter of fact, the snowball got its song heard and it was "on hold" for Alan Jackson for three weeks. Why? Because the snowball was in a music center! You need to be there, too.

We know, we know, there is a publisher in your town who knows the second cousin of the gardener whose next door neighbor is the brother-in-law of Faith Hill's bus driver. So does everyone else, even the snowball. You must get your songs heard by the people who count, and the people who count are in major music centers.

COMMITMENT:
In order to move closer to getting my first cut,
*I will visit a major music center at least three times a year
to attend and play writer's nights, co-write, and network.*

______________________________					______________________________
            Date																				Signed

Now keep in mind that visiting three times a year is the <u>goal</u>. You don't have to visit three times <u>this</u> year. *For now, let's just work on making <u>one</u> visit happen.*

So how do you get there from where you are when you only have a two week vacation, summer is coming and the kids want to go to Disney World in Orlando? Or, you just maxed out your MasterCard on a new 100,000 mhz iMac OSXXI? Or, your agoraphobia has suddenly returned at the thought of walking into the Warner-Chappell office only to face a tape copy boy named Vinny. Don't worry. We were expecting that. Stay with us.

<u>SELECTING A TARGET CITY</u>

First you need to decide where you are going. While every music center addresses all types of music, they each have their own styles on which they focus better than others. Do you write rock, pop or R&B? L.A. is probably your choice. Country, Contemporary Christian & Gospel are easy. Nashville's your place. Eclectic rock, jazz, R&B and show tunes make New York your destination.

 <u>DECIDING ON YOUR TARGET CITY AND DATE</u>
After much mulling and advice-seeking from peers in clubs, organizations and music stores in your area, write down the city you think best fits your songwriting style:

Target city: ____

Now grab a #2 pencil with an eraser and your Far Side calendar and pick some possible dates that would work that are at least two months away:

Target dates: ____

Depending on the music center you're visiting, there are many activities that may interfere with those dates. You need to be aware of them, so before we finalize a date, we have some more homework to do. Go to the appropriate city heading then do the exercises contained within.

<u>RESEARCHING A DATE FOR YOUR VISIT</u>

IF YOUR TARGET CITY IS LOS ANGELES
There's always something going on in Los Angeles. Even when there isn't, they want you to think there is. There are some times, however, that you <u>do</u> need to avoid: The Academy Awards, the Grammys, the Academy of Country Music Awards, Midem, and earthquakes above 4.2 on the Richter scale. Call the Academy of Motion Picture Arts and Sciences, the National Academy of Recording Arts and Sciences or the ACM to find out when their events are scheduled, or you can check the internet. These organizations are listed in the appendix at the end of this workbook.

<u>RESEARCHING LOS ANGELES EVENTS</u>
Research these organizations and fill in below:
1. According to The Academy of Motion Picture Arts and Sciences, the next upcoming Academy Awards (Oscars) are scheduled for________________________.
1. According to the National Academy of Recording Arts and Sciences, the next upcoming Grammy Awards are scheduled for___________________________________.
1. According to the Academy of Country Music, the next upcoming ACM Awards are scheduled for_________________________.
1. According to Midem, the next upcoming International Music Festival is scheduled for_____________________.

IF YOUR TARGET CITY IS NASHVILLE

In Nashville, the week of the CMA Awards, Fan Fair, and Country Radio Seminar (CRS) Week, are events that take up time and energy from the people you're trying to get to. It's next to impossible to get to them. Call the CMA, and find out when the awards are scheduled. While you're talking to them ask about Fan Fair too. Call Radio & Records Magazine and find out when CRS Week is. South By Southwest in Austin has been drawing a lot of attention from Nashville, too. If you want to save on your long distance bills, check out these organization's websites. They are all in the appendix.

RESEARCHING NASHVILLE EVENTS

Research these organizations and fill in below:

1. According to the Country Music Association, the next upcoming CMA awards are scheduled for_______________________________.
2. According to the Country Music Association, the next upcoming Fan Fair is scheduled for_______________________________.
3. According to Radio and Records Magazine, the next upcoming Country Radio Seminar is scheduled for_______________________________.
4. According to SXSW, Inc, the next upcoming South By Southwest Music Conference is scheduled for_______________________________.
5. According to the Gospel Music Association, their next annual convention and Dove Awards are scheduled for _______________________________.

IF YOUR TARGET CITY IS NEW YORK

It's true; New York never sleeps. And neither will you if you go there at the wrong time. Sometimes the Grammys are held in New York. The World Series always seems like it's there. Fortunately there are few activities, save the Midem event and the CMJ Music Marathon (college music), to work your schedule around.

RESEARCHING NEW YORK EVENTS

Research these organizations and fill in below:

1. According to the CMJ Network, the next upcoming CMJ Music Marathon is scheduled for_______________________________.
2. According to Midem the next upcoming International Music Festival is scheduled for_______________________________.
3. According to the National Academy of Recording Arts and Sciences, the next upcoming Grammy awards in New York are scheduled for_______________________________.

Always remember that in all music centers certain holidays make the business off limits. Once there was a visitor to the NSAI office on the Wednesday before Thanksgiving. He was Canadian and didn't realize Music Row had shut down for the next four days. Keep in mind that generally from Thanksgiving to New Year's most businesses run on a limited schedule, and it's usually not a good time to try to make inroads then. Additionally, most people take their vacations in the summer, and the same goes for the music industry. And it seems everyone else who's trying to get into the music business goes to a music center during *their* summer vacation. Although summer is not an entirely horrible time to visit, there *are* better alternatives.

When American government holidays fall on Mondays (such as Memorial Day, Labor Day, etc.), businesses will generally also shut down the previous Friday.

Do any of the dates you investigated interfere with what you jotted down in your Far Side calendar? Scratch those out. If you have some dates still remaining, you've narrowed it down. If not, at least now you know when <u>not</u> to visit. Now let's find out some <u>good</u> dates to go.

There are a lot more good times than bad. After Jan 1st, everyone is kicking into high gear and listening for songs. Winter is also a good time because it's less competitive. Fewer people like to pitch their songs in a snowstorm – more opportunity for you. Fall is good as long as it's not around CMA Awards week. Artists are actively looking for songs. Publishers are actively pitching. The same goes for the spring.

There are some even more positive sides. Industry organizations schedule many events throughout the year that would be great for your first visit. NSAI holds its Spring Symposium in conjunction with its Tin Pan South songwriters' festival. The Nashville chapter of the Songwriters Guild (SGA) holds their "Songmania" almost once a month, and they host a "Building A Songwriting Career" workshop once a year in addition to "SGA Week" every February. With all that, let's go find a <u>good</u> time for you.

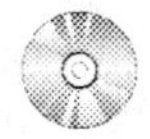RESEARCHING WORKSHOPS, EVENTS AND ACTIVITIES IN YOUR TARGET CITY
Contact the Songwriters Guild, BMI, ASCAP and SESAC in your target city, the Nashville Songwriters Association (if you're going there), the National Academy of Popular Music in New York as well as Women In Music in New York if that's where you are heading. Inquire as to any workshops, events or activities that would enhance your visit and lean you toward visiting on those dates. Use the notes page at the end of this chapter to jot info down. (Numbers and websites are in the appendix.) List the events and dates below that pertain to your target city:

	Sponsoring Organization	Event	Date
1.			
2.			
3.			
4.			
5.			
6.			

Now, do any of the above dates match the ones in your Far Side calendar?

Armed with information from one or more of the previous exercises, such as when you shouldn't go and when it's a good time to go, you should now have a specified date for your trek.

SETTING A TARGET DATE

DECIDNG ON A TARGET DATE
My target date for my first (or next) visit to a major music center is: ________________.

Whew! That took a lot! Give yourself a break and go write an up-tempo hit for The Backstreet Boys.

OK. The city is decided and the date is set. Now you gotta get there.

No, we haven't forgotten that we said we'd help you do that. If you still need some help, here are some ideas to get you closer with some other maybe less obvious avenues for you to travel.

- - - - -

➔ Remember the songwriting organization that you're now active in? Is it possible to schedule a "field trip" with other songwriters in your group? Some groups do so frequently. Some trips are merely for fact-finding, getting oriented, visiting open mics and writer's nights around town, and generally feeling comfortable with the environment. It's a great idea for a first trip. Others take it a step further and meet as a group with publishers, pro writers and other industry professionals.

See if your group might want to undertake the challenge. It's nice to travel with kindred spirits and share thoughts and experiences together. You can also address the money issue here by looking into group rates at hotels, splitting gas and several late-night group pizzas. (You want that last piece?)

- - - - -

➔ Here's another approach that may work for you. If the kids are driving you nuts for a family getaway, consider taking them to a music center this year instead of Six Flags Over Nebraska. There's plenty to entertain them in L.A., N.Y. or Nashville while you take a day or two to scope out the city. At the end of the day they will be dying to tell you stories about their ride on the Matterhorn at Disneyland, or seeing the dinosaur with feathers at the American Museum of Natural History or their daylong excursion at Nashville Shores while you were laying the groundwork to familiarize yourself with the business landscape.

Research the major music centers' tourist information and list fun family activities offered in each city to present to your family members. A good starting point would be checking out the visitor's bureau website for your target city in the appendix.

- - - - -

➔ Still need some ideas? Your first trip doesn't have to be a marathon. Do you have some comp time, sick leave or vacation days floating around your workplace that you have to use up? If so, a four-day weekend, Friday through Monday, may be just right for your adventure.

- - - - -

➜ Here's one more. Does your business have any clients, companies, or stores in your target center that need attention? Volunteer to be the good guy to go trouble-shoot there. You'll get major points for the effort and not have to sacrifice any company time while you call some of your music connections after you have taken that client to breakfast to let her know what a great job she's doing.

POTENTIAL MUSIC CENTER WORK-RELATED CONTACTS

List music center names, companies and phone numbers that your workplace does business with along with a reason to visit them. Make a proposal to your supervisor.

Company   Contact Name   Phone #

____

____

____

____

____

____

____

- - - - -

Remember we just said that visiting three times a year is the <u>goal</u>. All we're doing right now is putting one visit together. Then you can work on the next.

Your next step is to organize yourself before you leave. Notice in the survey question there are three categories: 1) attend and play writer's nights, 2) co-write, and 3) network. Let's start with organizing #1 - attending and playing writer's nights.

1. ATTENDING AND PLAYING WRITER'S NIGHTS

Writer's nights and open mics are the core of activity of the songwriting community. Besides providing a chance to be heard where you can perform old songs and test out new ones, they offer writers a sense of camaraderie and a place to commiserate with each other. There is an indescribable sense of creative spirit at these events, and that's what we want you to tap into.

The "attending" part of this category is intended for you to listen to what's going on and get an idea of your level of ability, where you fit in and where you need improvement. Eventually, however, attending is not enough. It's too easy to sit in the back of the room and listen to some other writer putting his songs on the line while you sit back and say to yourself, "I'm better than that".   That's where the "playing" comes in. You have to prove it.

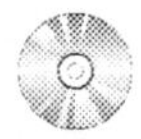 ## ORIGINAL SONGS TO PLAY OUT

List five original songs that you can perform in front of an audience without making more than two mistakes per song. (We know Bob Dylan forgets his lyrics occasionally, but he's singing in front of an adoring crowd who've come to expect it. You're not Bob – yet.) If you're not able to put any songs on this list, now is the time to start practicing. Once you feel comfortable with a couple of songs (translation: you can play them in the dark), list them below.

1. ____
2. ____
3. ____
4. ____
5. ____

RESEARCHING WRITER'S NIGHTS

Now it's time to find out where those open mics and writer's nights are so you can sing these babies. Go to your target city below, research it and track your information in the chart that follows the city listings.

IN LOS ANGELES:

Contacting the Songwriters Guild in L.A. is your best bet here as they are very active in this category. Also, as in Nashville, BMI, ASCAP and SESAC may be hosting writer's showcases. Numbers and websites are in the appendix.

Obtain a copy of the latest "LA Weekly" to find a listing of venues which host acoustic music nights, open mics and writer's nights. They also list "pay for play" venues, which your friendly authors won't endorse, but you may want to check them out for listening purposes anyway. You can also log on to www.laweekly.com, then click on "calendar" and then pick your music styles to find clubs that fit. It's a terrific site that has information on many, many open mics. Phone numbers are in the appendix.

Music Connection Magazine is a bi-weekly Los Angeles publication focusing on the music business. It's a great publication that while even though it's concentration is in L.A., it does an excellent job of monitoring the business in Nashville and New York. They also offer a once-a-year publication that lists L.A.'s venues that may serve your interests in performing. You can also log on to www.musicconnection.com, and click on "Nightlife" and/or "Songworks" for up-to-date info. And guess what? Phone numbers, etc. are in the appendix.

IN NASHVILLE:

Go to the NSAI website at www.nashvillesongwriters.com and click on the "open mic" page. There you will find an up-to-date listing of writer's nights and open mics complete with contact names and phone numbers.

You may also contact the Nashville chapter of the Songwriters Guild, BMI, ASCAP, and SESAC, as these organizations sometimes host their own writer's showcases in which you may be able to participate. Their phone numbers with contact names, along with website addresses, can be found in the appendix of this workbook.

Obtain a copy of the latest "Nashville Scene" and "Rage Entertainment Guide" by calling them for their distribution points to pick one up. (Note: they are available at the NSAI office.) Again, phone numbers and websites are in the appendix.

<u>IN NEW YORK</u>:

Contact the New York Regional NSAI Workshop for an up-to-date listing of performance venues. You should also call New York's SGA offices as well as BMI, ASCAP, and SESAC for their schedules.

Contact the National Academy of Popular Music in New York. They are a terrific group actively promoting songwriters and hosting open mics and showcases on a regular basis. You can log on to www.songwritershalloffame.org. Click on "Network Meetings and Open Mics" and "Showcases". Highly recommended.

Finally, in New York, call Women In Music for their schedule of performance showcases and see if you can be worked in. You can log on to www.womeninmusic.com and click on "Events Calendar". You also might also want to check their "Mentoring Program" and "Careers" page.

As usual, all numbers and sites of the resources named above are in this book's appendix.

 WRITER'S NIGHTS IN YOUR TARGET CITY
You've got a ton of info here. Let's use it. List below 5 writer's and/or open mic nights in your target city. Once you arrive, prove to us you **attended** them by writing in the date you went:

Venue: _______________________ Address: ___________________________ Date: ________
Venue: _______________________ Address: ___________________________ Date: ________
Venue: _______________________ Address: ___________________________ Date: ________
Venue: _______________________ Address: ___________________________ Date: ________
Venue: _______________________ Address: ___________________________ Date: ________

SCHEDULING WRITER'S NIGHTS
Now it's time to *play* those writer's and/or open mic nights. Thought you were going to get out of it, didn't you? Call and arrange to play. Again, once you arrive, prove to us you **played** them by writing in the date you performed:

Venue: _______________________ Phone: ___________________________ Date: ________
Venue: _______________________ Phone: ___________________________ Date: ________
Venue: _______________________ Phone: ___________________________ Date: ________
Venue: _______________________ Phone: ___________________________ Date: ________
Venue: _______________________ Phone: ___________________________ Date: ________

OK, now that wasn't so bad was it? You're on your way. Now it's time to get ready for those co-writing sessions when you arrive.

2. CO-WRITING

 <u>FAVORITE UNWRITTEN SONG TITLES</u>

Remember that list of unwritten song titles you organized in your computer back in Chapter 5? Print it out and put it in your suitcase. After you arrive in your music center and have met a writer from Topeka who wants to co-write with you, you'll remember where your song title list is. It's in your suitcase! Just for fun, list your 5 favorite titles below from that list.

1. ____
2. ____
3. ____
4. ____
5. ____

Now you have some song ideas ready to co-write. Remember those co-writing skills you developed in Chapter 3? Go back and look it over. Once you've played a couple of open mics and heard a few other talented writers in your target city, do some approaching and be approachable.

Okay. You're ready to attend, ready to play and ready to co-write. Your date is set, your songs are ready, and co-writers are waiting. Now let's get ready to <u>network</u> *before* you arrive.

3. NETWORKING

As we begin to develop your contacts, be aware of the fact that there are a hundred more of you at this very moment trying to get through the same doors. Always approach the folks behind the doors with courtesy and consideration of their busy schedule and be appreciative of the time they give to you. (Now don't get bent out of shape about those other 100 writers. You have a distinct advantage over them. In addition to the great songs you have, you are organized and prepared. They aren't. They don't have this workbook.)

We know you can perform those great songs of yours, but you need to have them on tape or CD now to get ready for the networking you'll be doing when you arrive.

 <u>DEMOED SONGS</u>

List below five solo written or co-written songs you have at least guitar/vocal good quality demos for. They can be the same five you have practiced for those writer's nights.

1. ____
2. ____
3. ____
4. ____
5. ____

<u>A WORD ON DEMOS</u>. If we had a dollar for every chapter, book, discussion, panel, seminar or question asked about demos, we wouldn't be waiting for our next royalty check. Simple or full? Songs have been cut from guitar/vocals, and from 10 piece band demos. Male or female? Songs have been cut from both sides here.   Most of the time the lyric will tell you. 4 or 24 track? The more there are, the bigger the dent in your wallet. The debate will go on long after you get your first check.

While there are no easy answers, there are some thoughts to consider. <u>First</u>, do not spend any money on a demo until you are absolutely, positively sure the song is ready. There's nothing worse than having a great demo on an incomplete song. Get feedback. Lots of it. Take advantage of evaluation services from songwriting organizations. Ask your co-writers for opinions. Maybe you even know a professional who is willing to mentor you and listen from time-to-time before you demo. <u>Second</u>, consider the song style. If it's a ballad, chances are you can have good luck with guitar or piano/vocal. If it has a groove - r&b, island, or heavy rock – you're going to need a band. <u>Third</u>, get the best musicians and singers possible (regardless of the demo's complexity). Chances are your wife's brother-in-law who plays Pizza Pizzaz every other Sunday won't really do your song justice. If you can sing circles around Trisha Yearwood or make Eric Clapton jealous of your guitar skills, then demo away. If not, make sure your song gets the musicianship and vocals it deserves. <u>Finally</u>, be sure the vocals are up-front and easy to hear.

   <u>DEMO CHECKLIST</u>
Before you head to the studio, let's do a little checklist:

________ 1. The song has been evaluated and is ready to go.
________ 2. The song style is determined and a decision as to simple or full demo is made.
________ 3. The best musicians and singers available are booked with the studio.
________ 4. Once recorded, the vocals are easy to hear above the tracks.

Do your five demos fill the bill? Good. Now let's go find a place to put them.

<u>PERFORMANCE RIGHTS ORGANIZATIONS (PROs) – ASCAP, BMI & SESAC</u>

Performance Rights Organizations essentially are the collection agencies for songwriters and publishers. When you score your first cut, you're going to have to be a member of one of them. Every PRO has offices in major music centers. They all have membership departments in which some of their functions are to listen, advise and encourage writers to become members of their organization, so this is a good place to start.

Are you already a member of a PRO? If so, that's great. But if not, don't worry. As a matter of fact, it could be to your advantage right now *not* to be a member. It doesn't hurt to be able to visit all three, seek out their industry advice and the advantages to becoming a member of their organization. They are all good people and worth checking out.

SETTING UP PERFORMANCE RIGHT'S ORGANIZATION APPOINTMENTS

List the names, addresses and phone numbers of the PROs in your target music center. Call each of them one month in advance of your visit, and ask for the membership department, noting the names of each person you speak with starting with the receptionist who answers the phone, all the way to your final contact. (You can use the blank "notes" pages at the end of this chapter.)

Once you've reached your final contact, explain that you are a songwriter coming to visit on such and such a date, that you are not a member of a PRO (unless you are, then of course say you are) and that you would like to set up an appointment to play a couple of songs and discuss the advantages of joining. (When leaving a voice mail message, always give in order: your name, phone number, who referred you, where you're staying, how long you're in town and your songwriting accomplishments. Ralph Murphy at ASCAP says, "Keep your message under 20 seconds.")

Bring in your three best songs (from your demo list on page 63) and be on time. Good luck.

BMI
Address: ____
Phone: ____
Main Receptionist: ____
Membership Dept. Receptionist: ____
First Contact: ____
2nd Contact: ____
Appointment Date and Time: _______________With:_________________________

ASCAP
Address: ____
Phone: ____
Main Receptionist: ____
Membership Dept. Receptionist: ____
First Contact: ____
2nd Contact: ____
Appointment Date and Time: _______________With:_________________________

SESAC
Address: ____
Phone: ____
Main Receptionist: ____
Membership Dept. Receptionist: ____
First Contact: ____
2nd Contact: ____
Appointment Date and Time: _______________With:_________________________

SONGWRITING ORGANIZATIONS

Each major music center has several organizations staffed to serve songwriters' interests. See page 36 in Chapter 4.

In Nashville the Nashville Songwriters Association International (NSAI) and in Nashville, Los Angeles and New York, The Songwriters Guild of America (SGA) offer ongoing educational events throughout the year. Just like the PROs, they are good people, and these are good places to hang out and find out where the latest writer's nights are going on.

Whatever city you're planning to visit, plan to visit these offices. It's a good idea to first visit their website and learn all you can about the organization.

 ## CONNECTING WITH SONGWRITING ORGANIZATIONS

Now it's time for more phone calls to your target city's professional organizations. Just like you did with the PROs earlier, list the names, addresses and phone numbers of the songwriting organizations in your target music center. Call each of them one month in advance and ask for the membership department, noting the names of each person you speak with starting with the receptionist who answers the phone, all the way to your final contact. (If you still have room, use those "notes" pages in the back.)

Again, once you've reached your final contact, explain that you are a songwriter coming to visit on such and such a date, that you are not a member of their organization (unless you are, then of course say you are), and you would like to set up an appointment to discuss the advantages of joining, and if possible, to play a couple of songs. Also ask about any events, writer's nights, and any other activities that may be occurring during the dates of your visit.

Organization: ____
Address: ____
Phone: ____
Main Receptionist: ____
Membership Dept. Receptionist: ____
First Contact: ____
2nd Contact: ____
Appointment Date and Time: _______________With:_______________________
Event Dates, Times, Cost: ____
____
____
____

Organization: ______________________________________
Address: ______________________________________
Phone: ______________________________________
Main Receptionist: ______________________________________
Membership Dept. Receptionist: ______________________________________
First Contact: ______________________________________
2nd Contact: ______________________________________
Appointment Date and Time: ______________________With:__________________________
Event Dates, Times, Cost: ______________________________________
                                                  ____
                                                  ____
                                                  ____

Be mindful that the phones are constantly ringing in these offices and jobs and members are being tended to. Keep your questions and conversations short, and you'll go a long way.

If this is your first visit, there is plenty here in this chapter to keep you busy. With a little luck, one of the PROs may refer you to play your songs to a music publisher. Don't push them to do so. Let them come up with the bright idea. If they don't or won't, just remember this is your first visit. We'll get you to those publishers next time. Right now, we just want you to get your feet wet.

If you have already visited a music center, you are probably ready for your songs to get to that next step with some publishers. So how do you get to 'em? That's what Chapter 7 is about.

Allrighty then! You are now armed with an incredible arsenal of information and contacts. Let's quickly review them.

1. You have 5 songs you can sing and perform at a writer's night.
2. You have 5 songs demoed and ready to play.
3. You have song titles and ideas to co-write.
4. You have names of contacts at Performing Rights Organizations and songwriter's organizations (including any events they have told you about).

Have a great trip.

JV:

My first music center trip was to Los Angeles in the summer of 1983. I drove my 72 VW (36 mpg) from KC to LA while staying with friends in Tulsa, Dallas, Phoenix, and Albuquerque along the way (no motel bills). I stayed in Glendale, sleeping on the floor of a garage apartment of an old girlfriend. (Her new boyfriend had a *real* job.) I cooked a few hamburgers and cleaned up her place a lot in return for the free floor.

I attended a wealth of meetings, workshops, pitch-a-thons and open mics in the 6 weeks I was there and got an incredible education. I even wrote and co-wrote a few songs and made some friends in between. During one of the meetings sponsored by the then Songwriter's Resource Services, a publisher asked if I had ever tried Nashville as a place to pitch my songs. (A nice way of saying he wasn't interested, but thought provoking none-the-less.) That got me making plans for a "spring fling" to the Nash. I wrote and wrote and wrote some more to get ready. I used the postcard method to make a few publisher appointments and, upon arriving, attended every writer's night in existence along with a couple of workshops. And I made some more friends.

Both trips allowed me an education I could never have gotten back in Kansas City and laid the groundwork for a mindset toward writing and co-writing competitively as well as making future contacts that, through a tangled web, would eventually lead me to that first cut. I sold the VW a year later. It was a yellow convertible. Wish I had it now.

GH:

In 1999, I was living in Los Angeles and working as Director of Development for Mark Bryan, co-founder of The Artist's Way Workshops. Mark was hired by the Country Music Association to present an Artist's Way weekend seminar in Nashville for CMA members. While in the thick of negotiating, I said to Mark, "You *are* going to take me with you, aren't you?" and he replied that if the CMA would pick up the tab for my hotel, he would use his frequent flyer miles for my air travel. <grin>

Once I realized that I wasn't dreaming and I was actually going to Nashville, it dawned on me that I couldn't pitch my songs to publishers because I hadn't demoed any of them! I telephoned a publisher I met at a National Academy of Songwriters Expo and asked him to refer me to a studio in L.A. $1100 later, I had two songs on tape. With a little footwork in advance, I was able to make one pitch in person, drop off at two other publishers, and mail in (with a code on the envelope, of course) to another publisher. The in-person pitch and the mail-in pitch both passed but said I should feel free to send them more of my songs. The drop-offs never returned my follow up calls. As of today, I'm still submitting songs to the publisher that accepted my song by mail. One out of four, not bad for my first visit and a little effort!

* * * * *

From Jon Ims

"Many years ago Paul Craft went to Nashville's Station Inn to hear a bluegrass band. After hearing several songs he liked, Paul asked who wrote them. The bass player told him it was me and gave Paul my number. I was living in Denver at the time when my phone rang and Paul was on the other end asking to hear 'everything' I wrote. As I had been sending songs to Nashville for years with zero response and as I had been told so many times to only send 2 or 3 songs at a time, I reluctantly sent Paul a cassette of 24 songs. Although 'Falling Out Of Love' was in the middle of the second side, Paul heard it and called to ask permission to demo the song and pitch it.

"He made several demoes of the song with several different singers, one being Linda Davis. Paul pitched that version for two years to Reba McEntire who continued to like the song. She finally cut it on the 'Rumor Has It' album.

"Paul eventually sent the newly released CD to me in Denver and I wouldn't play it for 3 days. I couldn't believe Reba had cut one of my songs. My girlfriend finally convinced me to put it on the stereo and when it came on I was blown away. It was better than I thought it could ever be. I have to admit I got teared up upon hearing it.

"It was the fourth and final single off that album and I first heard it driving to a $100 gig at the 'Little Bear' in Evergreen, Colorado. I turned it up all the way.

"By the way, they misspelled my name on the first record. They wrote 'Imms.' I still get a chuckle from that."

-Jon Ims
BMI award-winning songwriter and recipient of the 1992 BMI Song Of The Year for Trisha Yearwood's "She's In Love With The Boy"

* * * * *

<u>Jon's advice to songwriters:</u>
"This has been on my refrigerator forever:
<u>'Press On</u>
Nothing in the world can take the place of persistence. Talent will not; nothing is more common than unsuccessful men with talent. Genius will not; un-rewarded genius is almost a proverb. Education alone will not; the world is full of educated derelicts. Persistence and determination alone are omnipotent.'"

NOTES

CHAPTER
7

YOU ACTIVELY DROP OFF CDS OR TAPES
OF YOUR SONGS TO A MUSIC CENTER PUBLISHER
WHO HAS AGREED TO LISTEN TO THEM

YOU ACTIVELY DROP OFF CDS OR TAPES OF YOUR SONGS TO A MUSIC CENTER PUBLISHER WHO HAS AGREED TO LISTEN TO THEM

This is where the benefits of your hard work start to kick in. If you've done enough footwork in Chapter 6, then you are ready for the payoff of a music center publisher agreeing to take a listen. If you haven't scored with a publisher in Chapter 6, don't panic. That's where we're going now. There's no mystery here. It's just a matter of persistence and patience, patience and persistence. Did we mention persistence and patience?

There's never been a time we know of when songwriters were parading in the streets or shouting from the rooftops, "It's so _easy_ out there! Every door is wide open!" That's because the truth is, it _isn't_ easy. Publishers are very busy people with an agenda to get songs that are already in their catalogs cut and keeping their paid staff writers happy by doing so. They also are trying to get a return on their investment.

It's true that it's hard to get attention if you are a new writer, but it's also true that the successful publisher occasionally listens to that unheard writer that just stepped off the bus. So let's go find them.

> **COMMITMENT:**
> In order to move closer to getting my first cut,
> *I will actively drop off CDs or tapes of my songs to a music center publisher*
> *who has agreed to listen to them.*

_______________________   _____________________________________

          Date   Signed

One of the most frequently asked questions we get is: How do I get my songs heard by a publisher? While there may be an infinite number of methods, the following suggestions are some of the best paths to follow.

<u>The Cold Call Method</u>

For some reason, many people think you can only succeed if you go through back doors. Not true. Front doors are a good way to go especially when everyone else is trying to sneak in the back. But before we go knocking, we're going to create a "Publisher Database".

Start by getting out the Yellow Pages for your target city, either from the public library or the internet, and look up "Music Publishers". It will be a long list but jot, copy or print it out. Another great resource is Music Row Magazine's Publishers Edition for Nashville (www.MusicRow.com), and/or Music Connection Magazine's Publisher Edition for L.A. (www.MusicConnection.com). Is your long distance service cheap? Let's hope so, because you are going to be on the phone for a while here. But before you call, you need to have your approach ready to go.

<u>Kinda like this:</u>
"Hello, my name is Charley Chorus. I'm a songwriter from Coral Gables, and I'm planning on being in town on September 23rd. Would it be possible to drop off one or two original songs for your consideration?"

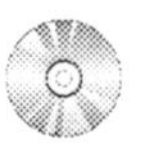 <u>CREATING YOUR APPROACH</u>
Get out a *separate* sheet of paper (or use the "note" page if you like) and write down a first draft of your *own* approach. Rehearse that approach into a tape recorder. How does it sound? If it needs improvement, do a rewrite. (Songs aren't the only things that need an occasional rewrite.) Rehearse again. Once you have the approach that you feel best represents you, write it down here:

____

____

____

____

____

Your approach and method is your own but always, always, <u>*always*</u> be kind, courteous and considerate.

If you decide to try this method, then one month in advance of your visit - beginning with "A" from the Yellow Pages you researched earlier - start calling. Use your most professional and courteous demeanor when the receptionist answers. Use your approach to tell him/her you are a songwriter planning to visit on such-and-such a date and request that you be permitted to drop off some songs to them.

They will probably say no. That's part of their job description. But don't hang up and accept defeat just yet. Say thank you, and ask if you may call at some distant date in the future. Even if they say no, write down their name. If they say yes, write down that future date and put it in your calendar. Use your "notes" page at the end of this chapter if you need to.

If they say yes, that you may drop off a tape or CD, ask to whose attention it should be addressed, and if you need to put a code on the outside. Write down that name and the code.

If they say yes, also ask for an appointment. They probably won't give you one, but you never know. They may even forward your call to someone (another name to write down).

 CREATING A PUBLISHER DATABASE
When you are done with that call, say thank you again and fill in the spaces below:

Publisher name, address and phone ____
____
Receptionist name: ____
Accepting songs?   Yes _____   No _____   How many? ______________________
If not, then in the future?   Yes _____   No _____   Maybe _____ When? ________________
Drop off?   Yes _____   No _____   Attention: ___________Code________
Appointment?   Yes _____   No _____
Date, time & with whom? ____
Additional contact name ____

Now that wasn't so bad, was it? Feel like another? Good. Here we go. Go ahead and photocopy the following publisher database on the next page as many times as necessary to keep your information intact. You may want to do this exercise with 3 x 5 cards, alphabetizing and flagging the positive responses for future reference. If you have a good database program in your computer, you can organize it there. Just make sure to bring your laptop with you or print it out before you arrive in your music center.

Publisher Database

Publisher name, address and phone ______________________________________

____

Receptionist name: ____
Accepting songs?   Yes _____   No _____   How many? ________________________
If not, then in the future?   Yes _____   No _____   Maybe _____ When? ________________
Drop off?   Yes _____   No _____   Attention: ______________Code________
Appointment?   Yes _____   No _____
Date, time & with whom? ____
Additional contact name ____

Publisher name, address and phone ______________________________________

____

Receptionist name: ____
Accepting songs?   Yes _____   No _____   How many? ________________________
If not, then in the future?   Yes _____   No _____   Maybe _____ When? ________________
Drop off?   Yes _____   No _____   Attention: ______________Code________
Appointment?   Yes _____   No _____
Date, time & with whom? ____
Additional contact name ____

Publisher name, address and phone ______________________________________

____

Receptionist name: ____
Accepting songs?   Yes _____   No _____   How many? ________________________
If not, then in the future?   Yes _____   No _____   Maybe _____ When? ________________
Drop off?   Yes _____   No _____   Attention: ______________Code________
Appointment?   Yes _____   No _____
Date, time & with whom? ____
Additional contact name ____

Publisher name, address and phone ______________________________________

____

Receptionist name: ____
Accepting songs?   Yes _____   No _____   How many? ________________________
If not, then in the future?   Yes _____   No _____   Maybe _____ When? ________________
Drop off?   Yes _____   No _____   Attention: ______________Code________
Appointment?   Yes _____   No _____
Date, time & with whom? ____
Additional contact name ____

 <u>INVITATIONS TO DROP OFF SONGS</u>

List below the publishers' names, addresses and phone numbers who invited you to drop off songs.

<u>Publisher Name</u>   <u>Phone #</u>   <u>Address</u>

____

____

____

____

One week before your visit, call them again to confirm that it's still ok to drop off your songs. And now, by the way, you have a name to ask for. Cool, huh?

Maybe you're a little behind in your AT&T payment, or maybe you have a long distance block on your phone, or maybe you're a little too shy to make these calls. Don't worry. Here's another tried and true method that Jerry used on his first visit to Nashville while still living in Kansas City.

<u>The Postcard Method</u>

<u>CREATING A PUBLISHER POSTCARD</u>

Just like in the "Cold Call Method" above, one month in advance of your visit, get out the Yellow Pages for your target city either from the public library or the internet and look up "Music Publishers". It will be a long list but jot, copy or print it out.

Go to your neighborhood post office, buy some postcards or get a stack of 4x6 index cards at your local Offices R Us, and either go to a printer or use your computer to print the following on the back of the card:

<table>
<tr><td>

_______ **Yes, you may drop off a tape or cd with no more than**

_______ **songs.**

_______ **Yes, you may come in and play no more than ___ songs.**

Date and time____

_______ **Sorry, we are not accepting outside songs right now.**

Contact name and phone #_______________________________________

</td></tr>
</table>

Now compose a letter like the one below:

Date

Twang & Tears Music
800 Music Circle North
Nashville, TN 37299
Attn: Joe Publisher

Dear _______________:

I am a songwriter from ____________________ planning on visiting __[music city]______
on _[date]______________. Would it be at all possible to bring some of my songs to
you then? A self-addressed, stamped postcard is included for you to check off your
response and drop in the mail.

Thank you,

Hit songwriter
888 Fender Road
Guitar Town, TX 11111
(555) 634-5789

IMPORTANT: In the upper left corner of the address side of the postcard, write in the name of
the publisher. It would be very disheartening to have a card come back inviting you to play your
songs and not knowing where it came from. (This happened to someone who will remain nameless).
Take those cards, stamp them (if they need to be), put your address on the front, stuff them in
your letter, put the letter in a business envelope, address it, and with the proper postage sling
'em in the mailbox.

Most of your cards will not be returned to you at all. Chalk it up as an investment. But if you are
lucky, you'll get 5 to 10 positive returns out of 100. But hey, all you need is one, right? Never
forget that.

TRACKING POSTCARD RESPONSES

As your postcards come back (give it two weeks or so), list below the publishers' names, addresses and phone numbers who invited you to drop off songs.

<u>Publisher Name</u>   <u>Phone #</u>   <u>Address</u>

____
____
____
____
____
____
____
____

Bring all this information with you the next time you head out to your favorite music center. Once you arrive, courteously take those CDs in.

Don't forget you are professional and businesslike when you drop off your songs -- just like you were when you made the initial phone call. We know it's scary to wonder what someone else is thinking about your music, but try to enjoy it by appreciating the fact you are in the game. If you got a check beside "plays well with others" on your second grade report card, you'll do great. Good luck!

So what do you do now with those postcards and/or agreements from publishers who have invited you to come for an in-person appointment? This is the chapter for drop offs. We'll deal with those appointments in the next chapter. Right now, we're getting you ready to begin those all-important relationships.

JV:

I had been in town a month and decided it was time to face the music. Making as many businesslike cold calls to publishers as I could, I was surprised to find several agreeing to listen to drop-offs. A few requested that I also leave an SASE in case I wanted the tape returned. So one weekday I dropped off about ten tapes. Then I waited for that phone to ring with a publisher calling and swearing I had just written Kenny Rogers' next single. What I got instead was one tape back in the mail. I noticed it hadn't been rewound, so out of curiosity I put it in the tape deck to see how far it had been heard. It was cut off after the very first line! The phone didn't ring that whole week. It gave me a lot of time to do some first line re-writes.

GH:

Prior to taking my first trip to Nashville, I had been given referrals from friends who knew publishers there. Before giving me their names and phone numbers, my friends called ahead and asked if it would be ok for me to give those publishers a call. Just a small amount of networking gave me those first four contacts. I still remember how exciting it was just walking down 16th Avenue that first time, knowing someone was willing to listen to my songs. It was enough to lift my feet off the ground.

* * * * *

From Steven Dale Jones

"My first cut on a major label was 'Paintin' The Town Blue' recorded by T. G. Shephard on Columbia Records in 1985. I had been writing for Rick Hall Publishing in Muscle Shoals at the time, and my song plugger played it for Rick who was producing T. G.

"I heard it through several stages of the song getting cut, mixed, remixed, adding strings, fixing the drum track and so on. Every time I heard a new version I was afraid it wouldn't make the album because they were going through so much trying to get it right that they would eventually give up on it. Fortunately, I was wrong, and, when the album came out, I went down to Pegasus Records in Florence, Alabama, to buy it. I tore it open and stared at my name at least a hundred times that day.

"I had promised myself that I would buy a Martin guitar with my first royalty check. After recoupment, my check wasn't quite enough to cover my Martin, but I got it anyway. I took a $139 and bought a thousand dollar guitar."

- Steven Dale Jones
ASCAP award-winning songwriter with over 80 songs recorded including "Ten Thousand Angels" by Mindy McCready and "I Know How The River Feels" and Grammy-nominated "One More Day" by Diamond Rio

* * * * *

<u>Steven's advice to songwriters:</u>
"If you do it for money or fame, it's never gonna work. You write because it's what you do, and the longer you do it, the greater the chance your number's gonna be called."

NOTES

CHAPTER
8

YOU HAVE PITCHED YOUR SONGS IN PERSON
TO A MUSIC CENTER PUBLISHER

YOU HAVE PITCHED YOUR SONGS IN PERSON
TO A MUSIC CENTER PUBLISHER

While it may be true that your songs sound better in person than they do if they were just dropped off, there is more going on than just a song in an appointment. We are going to say this many times throughout this workbook, so get it chiseled into that gray matter up there:

The music business is a business of relationships.

It's a lot easier to develop a relationship in person than it is when you're just dropping off a song. You have already developed the skills to contact music publishers in a professional and business-like manner. We're going to use those skills here, expand them, and in addition, we're going to start developing those all-important relationships.

☞ COMMITMENT:
In order to move closer to getting my first cut,
I will pitch my songs in person to a music center publisher.

______________________   ______________________________
            Date   Signed

From all your hard work in Chapters 6 and 7, you now have more clout to take a more professional and business-like approach. You no longer are a newcomer. You have some folks listening and maybe even pitching a few of your tunes. But before you make any calls (we'll get there in a moment), we are going to get ready to use your current contacts to make more contacts. We are going to use an approach similar to that in Chapter 7, but with more content now. Look over this mock "sales pitch":

"Hello. My name is Tanya Twang. I'm a songwriter from Tulsa. I have songs being pitched by XYZ Publishing and Sara Songplugger at Drop-In-The-Bucket Music. I've also been working on a regular basis with Roger O'Leary at BMI. I'm coming into town in a month and would like an opportunity to open more doors and play some songs for you." (This is the approach that Jerry used many times and he was rarely turned down.)

CREATING A SALES PITCH

Get out a *separate* sheet of paper and write down a first draft of *your own* sales pitch. Include the names of the publishers and PRO representatives with whom you are working. Rehearse that sales pitch into a tape recorder. How does it sound? If it needs improvement, do a rewrite. (Songs aren't the only things that need an occasional rewrite.) Rehearse again. Once you have the sales pitch that you feel best represents you, write it down here:

____

____

____

____

____

____

____

____

____

____

MAKING TRAVEL PLANS

Now write down the date of your next planned visit: ____________________________________.

INVITATIONS FROM PUBLISHERS

Now list below the publishers who invited you for a sit-down appointment from those previous post cards, phone calls and/or referrals:

Publisher: Phone Number:

_______________________________   _______________________________

_______________________________   _______________________________

_______________________________   _______________________________

_______________________________   _______________________________

_______________________________   _______________________________

_______________________________   _______________________________

CALLING YOUR PRO REP

Call your representative at your PRO. (Remember, that's your Performance Rights Organization – ASCAP, BMI or SESAC.) Have a frank discussion with him about your songs and your progress. Ask if he will make some phone calls to publishers on your behalf. If he agrees, follow up at an agreed future time to find out whom he has contacted. Once he has, list them with their phone numbers here:

Publisher: Phone Number:

___________________________   ___________________________

___________________________   ___________________________

___________________________   ___________________________

___________________________   ___________________________

___________________________   ___________________________

___________________________   ___________________________

___________________________   ___________________________

REVIEWING PUBLISHERS' RESPONSES

Refer back to the results of your postcards, phone calls and PRO referrals and dig out your "Publisher Database" from Chapter 7. First, list the good guys who let you drop off songs to them. Next, earmark all the ones that initially said "no" to your request or never even answered your request to have your songs heard. Also earmark those "drop-offs" that passed or that you never heard back from. List all those names and phone numbers here:

Publisher: Phone Number:

___________________________   ___________________________

___________________________   ___________________________

___________________________   ___________________________

___________________________   ___________________________

___________________________   ___________________________

___________________________   ___________________________

 ## MAKING APPOINTMENTS WITH PUBLISHERS

Now call the above publishers in this order: The ones who initially agreed to an appointment, the ones referred by your PRO representative and finally all the leftovers. Set an appointment using your rehearsed "sales pitch" established earlier. List all the appointments you've secured here:

Publisher: ____

Date: _________________________________ Time: ___________________________

Publisher: ____

Date: _________________________________ Time: ___________________________

Publisher: ____

Date: _________________________________ Time: ___________________________

Publisher: ____

Date: _________________________________ Time: ___________________________

Publisher: ____

Date: _________________________________ Time: ___________________________

Put the above appointments in your personal calendar, appointment book or, for you 21st Century types, your PalmPilot.

While it isn't possible to teach someone to be personable and friendly, there are some "do's and don'ts" to consider while you are sitting across the desk from the person who is about to make some decisions that may affect your livelihood. It can be uncomfortable at best and frightening at worst to have someone listen to your new creations and wonder what they are thinking, let alone hear that it doesn't move them. But remember that these people are all nice folks who really have no intention of hurting your feelings. In fact, they would like nothing more than to find the next "Change The World" coming out of their speakers. But as business people, they know that they have to make tough decisions that deal with creativity. That's where smiles and thick-skin development come in for you (don't go running to the dermatologist).

 ## TEN COMMANDMENTS OF PROFESSIONAL ETIQUETTE

Look over the ten suggestions below and consider them <u>before</u> you go into your appointment. When you return, check them off if you remembered to use them:

Appt. 1   Appt. 2   Appt. 3

_____   _____   _____   1.   Show up on time.
_____   _____   _____   2.   Put your strongest song first on your CD/tape.
_____   _____   _____   3.   Pitch a maximum of three songs.
_____   _____   _____   4.   Have three more ready (but only if requested).
_____   _____   _____   5.   Be quiet and listen.
_____   _____   _____   6.   Don't argue, get angry or huffy.
_____   _____   _____   7.   Don't suggest to the publisher that he go back and listen to the cool four minute plus fade right after he cut it off at the end of the first chorus.
_____   _____   _____   8.   Don't point out their fallacies (even when they say something stupid).
_____   _____   _____   9.   Say "Thank you" (and mean it) after the end of your appointment.
_____   _____   _____   10.   Say "Thank you" and smile at the receptionist. (Mean that, too.)

After three appointments, if you don't have it down pat, upgrade your dose of gingko biloba. If you don't have any, go to your kids' school, sneak into the social studies classroom after hours and write 100 times on the blackboard: "I will always mind my manners".

 ## PRACTICING YOUR PUBLISHER APPROACH

You probably won't do this, but we suggest you find a friend who still resents losing that Monday Night Football bet to you. Tell him he gets to play the evil publisher who can cut off your songs early, yawn during their playback, read the newspaper and answer the phone in the middle of the first verse. He can also say he likes one of your songs if he really does. Set up a mock office in your apartment complete with a boom box and stacks of unsolicited cassettes on the desk. No, really. Take this seriously. Set up your CD or tape with 3 songs on it. Knock on the door, enter in a friendly and professional manner, shaking hands and complimenting his paisley shirt. Give him the CD and practice the Ten Commandments of Professional Etiquette suggestions in the previous section. The purpose of this exercise is to have already experienced the worst. When you experience it in real life where it counts, it will be a piece of cake. Chocolate. Have fun, but try to get a sense of the reality of the situation. Besides, when you really <u>are</u> in that appointment, you can think back on this role-play and smile.

 <u>SENDING THANK YOU CARDS</u>

Stockpile a box of simple thank you cards. Once you've had your appointment, take one out and jot down a short note saying thanks for the appointment. Write below the publisher's name and the date you sent the card.

Publisher: Date Sent:

_______________________________   _______________________________
_______________________________   _______________________________
_______________________________   _______________________________
_______________________________   _______________________________
_______________________________   _______________________________
_______________________________   _______________________________
_______________________________   _______________________________

Above all, be positive and honest. Remember that the person you are talking to knows "Sara" and "Roger" (page 85) and at some time will bring your name up to them for discussion. If you're misrepresenting yourself, that door will never open again.

Probably the most important aspect of <u>any</u> relationship is just be yourself. That and a great song will take you a long way. Good luck again.

JV:
After making cold calls to them, two publishers agreed to hear my songs. I'm embarrassed to even think of the songs I took in, but instead of throwing me out and telling me to move back home, they were very kind and encouraging. I took notes. I listened to their helpful comments and relished in a compliment or two. I decided to be friendly without being squirrelly or brown-nosing. It worked. They said come back anytime. That was over 16 years ago. The first publisher is now an A&R rep at a major label and welcomes my songs regularly. And the second publisher? We signed an exclusive songwriter contract 15 years later. Sure glad I made those appointments!

GH:
Sitting across from someone listening to my songs is painfully scary for me. I have to sit there and do "self talk" inside my head the whole time they're listening. I tell myself things like, "inhale God, exhale fear, inhale God, exhale fear." If I don't do this then I end up watching them listening to my music while trying to second-guess what they're thinking. Not a good idea. It's a quick way to drive myself crazy. It has gotten easier with practice, and I just keep reminding myself that everything is in divine order!

* * * * *

From Steve Bogard

"In the early '70s I was in Memphis when I got word that a group on Dot/ABC records was coming there to record. The group was called 'The Travelling Magic' and they needed a song for their 'B' side. I told my co-writer that if we wrote a song with the word 'magic' in the title then maybe we'd have a shot at a cut, so we wrote one called "Touch Me With Magic They did cut the song, but I don't remember anything really happening with it.

"Twelve years later, I was in Miami producing TV and radio jingles while still writing songs. One day in the studio I happened to pick up a Billboard Magazine and I glanced at the Country Hot 100 singles chart. There on the charts was a song sung by Marty Robbins called 'Touch Me With Magic.' I called the publisher of the song to see if just maybe it was mine. It was! I couldn't believe it. Not only was I excited to have that cut, but I was even more thrilled that the legendary Marty Robbins was the one who did it. It went top 10 and was a BMI award-winning song.

"Marty's version of 'Touch Me With Magic' was the reason I came to Nashville to be a songwriter. It all started with that band in Memphis."

- Steve Bogard
BMI award-winning songwriter with numerous recordings including "Carried Away" by George Strait, "Prayin' For Daylight" by Rascal Flatts, and "Carryin' Your Love With Me" also by George Strait on the Grammy and CMA Album of the Year by the same title

* * * * *

<u>Steve's advice to songwriters</u>:
"Songwriting is a lot like when you are standing in a room trying to remember someone's name. You try to force it out, but it just won't come. Later, when you relax, it comes right up.
When you are writing, relax and let the song flow through you."

NOTES

NOTES

CHAPTER
9

YOU PERFORM YOUR SONGS EITHER SOLO OR IN A
GROUP OR BAND AT LEAST ONCE EVERY TWO
MONTHS IN A MAJOR MUSIC CENTER
(CLUBS AND/OR WRITER'S NIGHTS)

**YOU PERFORM YOUR SONGS EITHER SOLO OR IN A GROUP OR BAND
AT LEAST ONCE EVERY TWO MONTHS IN A MAJOR MUSIC CENTER
(CLUBS AND/OR WRITER'S NIGHTS)**

Up to now, we've been focusing on knocking on publishers' front doors to get your songs heard. That's not the only door for you to knock on. Every music center has a wealth of venues offering open mics, talent nights, writer's nights and even an occasional paying gig. You never know who will be in the audience that can have a positive effect on the success of your songs. Places to perform your material offer opportunities to be heard and to network.

Unless you're living in a grass hut in a Peruvian rain forest, surrounded by mosquito netting, and you're happy that your only audience is a bunch of squawking macaws (in which case you're not reading this book anyway, so it wouldn't matter), you can never have your songs heard too many times. Playing your songs out affords the opportunity to perfect your material, improve your performance and test out new songs on an audience. We already know your mother loves your songs, but when the guy who just slammed down three Millers at the bar stops and turns to listen to your three songs, it might be a good indication that you're on to something.

Playing out also offers networking opportunities that are different from sitting in a publisher's office. First of all, no one turns the song off after the first chorus. Secondly, publishers, A&R reps, publicists, artist managers and other vagabonds of the music business occasionally stray into open mics, writer's nights and gigs. Sometimes they show up because someone told them a good writer is performing, or sometimes they were invited. Sometimes they're just looking to finish off a margarita after a hard day at the office listening to songs. (Tough job, huh?). Additionally, these nights are frequented by potential artists looking to hear new songs and writers. Finally (and maybe most importantly), these venues are a home away from home for songwriters looking to expand their co-writing circle. And _you_ are the writer that all of the above are going to hear.

COMMITMENT:

In order to move closer to getting my first cut,
*I will perform my songs either solo or in a group or band
at least once every two months in a major music center.*

_______________________   _______________________
          Date   Signed

Once you have solidified the date of your next music center visit, start the work below.

 ## UPDATING WRITER'S NIGHT AND OPEN MIC VENUE INFO

Back in Chapter 6 you did extensive research on clubs, venues and organizations hosting writer's and open mic nights. Venues and schedules can change, so go back for a moment and update your research.

As a result of your updated research, list below five venues, contact names, phone numbers, time of the events, song limits, and the days of the week they schedule writer's nights and/or open mics:

Venue: ____

Phone: ____

Contact: ____

Day of week: _________________________________ Time: ___________________

Song Limit: ____

Venue: ____

Phone: ____

Contact: ____

Day of week: _________________________________ Time: ___________________

Song Limit: ____

Venue: ____

Phone: ____

Contact: ____

Day of week: _________________________________ Time: ___________________

Song Limit: ____

Venue: ____

Phone: ____

Contact: ____

Day of week: _________________________________ Time: ___________________

Song Limit: ____

Venue: ____

Phone: ____

Contact: ____

Day of week: _________________________________ Time: ___________________

Song Limit: ____

SCHEDULING GIGS

You have, of course, called the above and scheduled yourself in, right? Good. Now show us your schedule for the next two months. (Seem too much in advance? Not for many clubs, trust us.)

Month: Venue: Date/Time Scheduled:
____

____
____
____
____

Remember, your goal is a minimum of one performance every other month. If you can schedule in more, by all means do so.

GETTING AN AUDIENCE

Now let's bring some people in to hear you. For every month that you have a scheduled gig, list below your PRO rep, your established publisher contacts and your co-writers and tell them you are playing and would very much like it if they could break away to come hear you. You might entice your co-writer by telling her you'll be doing one of the songs the two of you wrote. (Make sure you always mention your co-writer's name, not only to stroke their ego, but also because it broadcasts to your audience that you have co-writing skills. That makes you available not only to new co-writers but to that next Grammy-winning artist that's there listening in the crowd.)

Name: Phone #:   Agreed to Attend (Yes/No/Maybe):
____
____
____
____
____
____
____
____

Allright. Now you're ready to go! Don't forget to practice and above all, have fun. Remember, this is really why you write in the first place -- to have your songs reach an audience.

Look back. Level two of the pyramid – - "Connecting To The Music Business" - - is now behind you! Keep climbing. You're getting stronger.

JV:

One night after playing the Bluebird, I was approached by a publisher to write with one of his staff writers. I, of course, was ecstatic to do so. That eventually led to a staff deal there for myself, which eventually led to my two Tim McGraw cuts. Once when I played Tin Pan South at the Radio Cafe, an A&R rep was there and asked me for a copy of a song. Once at a now-forgotten bar on Nashville's east side, a publisher asked for and signed one of my songs. Another time, I heard a kid play and asked him to sing a demo, then we wrote (and are still writing) a bunch of neat songs together. His name is Blake Shelton. I've met most of my co-writers, publishers, recording artists and most importantly, my friends by playing out. Don't ever ask me to play somewhere. I will.

GH:

Mark Irwin and Irene Kelley co-wrote a song entitled, "A Little Bluer Than That". Irene put it on her latest CD, which eventually was picked up by Relentless Records. But wait. The story doesn't end there. Irene played the song one night on the Grand Ole Opry. It just so happens that Alan Jackson was driving around in Nashville listening in to WSM-AM and loved the song. He searched out that one song and recorded it the next week. It's now on his latest album, "Drive". But wait. The story doesn't end there. Mark and Irene are two very happy songwriters, and Mark is especially happy that Irene likes to play that song at her gigs.

* * * * *

From Liz Hengber

"My very first major label cut was by Reba McEntire, 'For My Broken Heart.' I had been pitching songs to Starstruck Music, building a relationship with their Creative Manager, Clay Myers, and I played him that song in October 1990. He played the song for Reba, and she put it on hold for her next project. After she had lost her band in a tragic plane accident, Reba decided that recording that song would be the right thing to do, and she cut it in April of '91. Three months later I signed an exclusive contract with Starstruck Music.

"I was on my way to a writing appointment the first time I heard it on the radio. I just couldn't put my car into park. Instead, I drove by the old home I lived in while I was waiting tables and reflected back on those days, where I had been and where I was then, as I heard Reba singing. I couldn't cry because I still had a writing appointment to go to."

- Liz Hengber
ASCAP award-winning songwriter of four number one songs by Reba McEntire: "For My Broken Heart", "It's Your Call", "And Still" and "Forever Love". Liz also wrote "Unconditional" by Clay Davidson and "She's More" by Andy Griggs.

* * * * *

<u>Liz's advice to songwriters</u>:
"Believe in yourself and keep bringing those songs in. Include a couple of pecan pies. (Clay's favorite.)"

NOTES

CHAPTER
10

YOU LIVE
(AND FREQUENTLY PARTICIPATE
IN MUSIC INDUSTRY EVENTS)
WITHIN 100 MILES OF A MAJOR MUSIC CENTER

YOU LIVE (AND FREQUENTLY PARTICIPATE IN MUSIC INDUSTRY EVENTS) WITHIN 100 MILES OF A MAJOR MUSIC CENTER

Now don't start packing. Don't give your supervisor two weeks' notice. Don't tell your spouse to call your real estate agent or have your kids' transcripts sent to the Nashville school district. Don't move there just yet.

While it *is* true that many successful songwriters do not live in a major music center city, most of them visit so frequently that some business professionals actually think those writers are living there. Although you don't always have to be present to win, it does help. But don't move there yet.

The qualifying phrase in the statement above is "frequently participate in music industry events". You can live in a major music center, hide in a corner sheltering yourself from the realities of rejection and acceptance, and you will never get a cut. You might as well be living in Anchorage as in L.A. Just living there, then, isn't enough. You have to be involved, and for most people it's easier to be involved when you're in the middle of the creative beehive. But don't move there yet.

Here we go again: this is a business of relationships. While you are visiting three times a year and, in fact, establishing relationships, they are still relationships based on those three times a year. You aren't going to run into the MCA A&R rep at a grocery store in Boise. Your child isn't going to attend pre-school with a major recording artist's daughter in Albuquerque. If you're living in Duluth, you're not going to get invited to a post-CMA party by a publisher that you signed a single-song contract with in Nashville. But don't move there yet.

Okay. "Frequently Participate" (hereafter "FP") means really being involved more often than three visits a year. So instead of calling Mayflower Van Lines, let's just get you closer to FP status. As you become more involved in the business, it will be easier for you and your family to make a decision of whether or not to make the move. But it is still a decision that needs to be made with great care and consideration. So don't move there just yet.

Now don't get us wrong. If you're single, completely out of debt, have unlimited wealth stockpiled in the bank, your paid-for car still has its hundred thousand mile warranty in place, and your picture is not hanging in the post office, sure, go for it. You only have to answer to yourself and you've got nothing to lose. (But remember, it's your decision, not ours.)

Assuming you're making your three visits per year as established in Chapter 6, how do you get closer to FP status? There's really only one answer: <u>visit more often</u>. You'll soon discover that as the business is taking you more seriously and as you are taking your songwriting more seriously, three times a year won't get it done. There are a lot of networking and learning opportunities you can add to your already established routine. So let's start there. You already have your PRO contacts in place and you have publishers who are willing to listen to your songs on a regular basis when you're in town. Your next job is to expand your relationship base.

COMMITMENT:
In order to move closer to getting my first cut,
*I will work towards achieving "FP" status by increasing my visibility
and the frequency of my visits to a music center.*

_______________________   _______________________________
        Date   Signed

NEXT PLANNED VISIT

Write down the date of your next planned visit: ____.

Publishers, publishers, publishers. Is that all we're going to talk about? No! While they are one of the most important games in town, there are other games you need to play. You've already been dabbling in some others in previous chapters such as networking and playing your songs in public regularly. We are now going to take a look at industry events that not only help you keep building relationships (will we ever stop with this?), but also upgrade your education some.

Each music center offers a wealth of activities for you to participate in. You just have to find them and add them to your list next to co-writing, playing writer's nights, publisher appointments, etc. Let's go find them.

Go to the appropriate city heading in this chapter that addresses your target city, and then do the exercises following.

IF YOUR TARGET CITY IS LOS ANGELES

The Songwriters Guild offers several events in L.A. including, but not limited to, "Ask-A-Pro", "Becoming Remarkable", "Writing Music for Hit Songs", "Hit Songwriting" and "Song Styles".

ASCAP has workshops in "Film Scoring" and "Jazz", as well as others.

BMI offers a "Circles of Song Showcase" and "BMI 101" workshop, to mention a couple.

NARAS (National Academy of Recording Arts and Sciences) offers several networking opportunities via their membership meetings, "Professional Development" and "Educational Development" series. In addition, they have an "Up Close And Personal" workshop series and informal seminars such as "Get A Gig In The Music Biz".

There are also scores of industry showcases that you can find out about from your contacts.

IF YOUR TARGET CITY IS NASHVILLE

The Songwriters Guild offers many events such as "Song Critiques", "Ask-A-Pro", and "Building A Songwriting Career" workshops. Be sure to check out their monthly "Songmania" series and once-a-year miniature golf tournament.

ASCAP has its yearly membership meeting, "Ladies Golf Tournament and Tupperware Party", and the ASCAP Foundation workshops for songwriters.

BMI offers its monthly songwriting workshops, offering up-close examination of melodies, lyrics and structure.

NARAS (National Academy of Recording Arts and Sciences) has its annual membership meeting as well as a "Block Party" for members and their guests in the spring.

The CMA has its "CMA Forum" and their "Music City Tennis Invitational" in addition to its awards program.

NSAI offers "Tin Pan South Week" that includes their TPS Golf Tournament, Legends Concert and Spring Symposium as well as various club shows featuring upcoming and hit songwriters such as "The Bald and the Beautiful". Don't forget NSAI's weekly Thursday night workshops including "Pitch-to-Publisher" sessions, guest speakers, a "Pro Teaching" series and "Critique Nights".

Subscribers to Music Row Magazine can check out their calendar of events on their website.

And just as important, there are also scores of industry showcases that you can find out about from the contacts you have already made.

IF YOUR TARGET CITY IS NEW YORK

The Songwriters Guild has its "Song Critiques", "Street Smarts" and "Pro Shops" series.

ASCAP is busy with its "New York Music and Internet Expo", "Songwriters Circle", and "Producers In The Round Showcase".

BMI hosts its regular "Open Mics", and "Acoustic Roundup".

NARAS (National Academy of Recording Arts and Sciences) has membership meetings and various showcases.

There are also scores of industry showcases that you can find out about from the contacts you have already made.

All of the above are just samples of networking opportunities available to you. In all the target cities we found the information on each of the organizations' websites.

Go to the appendix to find out their websites to aid you in the following homework.

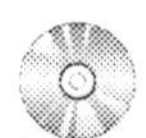 EVENTS CHART

After researching websites, publications, co-writers, friends and your Uncle Bert's roommate's ex-wife's second cousin who picks up Madonna's trash every other Wednesday (a songwriter, of course), fill in the following events chart that fits in with the date of your next scheduled visit to your music center and corresponds with each organization:

<u>Organization</u>   <u>Event</u>   <u>Date</u>

<u>Songwriters Guild</u> ____

<u>ASCAP</u> ____

<u>BMI</u> ____

<u>NARAS</u> ____

<u>CMA</u> ____

<u>NSAI</u> ____

If the date of your next visit is "event lacking'" reconsider a date with more opportunities.

 <u>SHOWCASES</u>

List below all the showcases you found out about by contacting your target city resources:

Venue: _________________________ Address: _______________________________________

Date/Time: ___________________ Featured Artist:_________________________________

Venue: _________________________ Address: _______________________________________

Date/Time: ___________________ Featured Artist:_________________________________

Venue: _________________________ Address: _______________________________________

Date/Time: ___________________ Featured Artist:_________________________________

Venue: _________________________ Address: _______________________________________

Date/Time: ___________________ Featured Artist:_________________________________

<u>EVENTS AND SHOWCASES NOTES</u>

Upon returning, record below the events you attended along with any names, phone numbers and notes you want to keep in mind (i.e., "Met Pete Potentialcowriter at a showcase at The Mint on Monday, 5/28. The band was called Blood. They sucked, but the lead singer was great. Her name was Buffy Baggins -- no relation to Bilbo -- and she sounded a little like Janis Joplin").

Event:____Date:____________________
Names/Numbers:____
Notes:____

____

Event:____Date:____________________
Names/Numbers:____
Notes:____

____

Event:____Date:____________________
Names/Numbers:____
Notes:____

____

If you've already made your three visits this year, it's time to make this visit # 4 - - and then #5 - - and then #6. Congratulations. You're moving into "FP" status.

We can't tell you if and when to make a permanent move to a major music center, but with each visit that you make, you will come closer to knowing what is right for you.

Your decision involves many factors that are unique to <u>you</u>. First and foremost is your family. Any decision this monumental **_MUST_** consider them and include their input. If the decision is not unanimous and/or there is hesitation or reluctance -- STOP. Think long and hard about this and reconsider. Remember what we said at first. You don't have to live in a major music center; it just helps. But don't move there yet.

JV:
I'll never forget the first time I walked into the Bluebird Sunday Writer's Night as a new Nashville resident. I had been in town a week, and, after busting my butt on a temp job, running out of gas in a thunderstorm and only having enough cash for a bag of potato chips to get me to the Tuesday paycheck, you could say I was a little homesick. A kind soul at the club struck up a conversation asking where I was from. I proceeded to moan about leaving my job, my girlfriend, my family, and my home, thinking I was pretty special. My new friend informed me that everyone in the room that night had done the same thing. It was a humbling revelation.

I can't say that I wouldn't have my first cut if I had stayed in Kansas City. I can't say that I am more successful as a writer because I'm here. But I <u>can</u> say without any qualification, that I am a better songwriter a hundred times over because I am in this incredible songwriting community. Being here raises your consciousness, your awareness and your sense of what you really have to do. And although sometimes that awareness is painfully overwhelming, I'm still glad I did it. Absolutely no regrets.

GH:
There's a part of me that loves shaking hands and talking to strangers. Then there's the side that loves to stay in and curl up with a good book. Unfortunately, when it's time to attend industry events I almost always feel like tucking in. So what do I do? I bargain. I take my curious self to the party then reward my inner-introvert by coming home and putting on sweats. Works every time.

At the very first NARAS block party that I attended, there were maybe three people I knew besides my co-workers. The next year when the block party rolled around again, I found myself looking forward to it. After one short year of attending industry events, everywhere I turned there was a friendly face. I felt like I was home (only without the sweats!).

---

* * * *

From Kirsti Manna

"My husband and I moved to Nashville from the Youngstown, Ohio area. In six months we had a Patty Loveless cut that didn't make the album. We never did get to hear it. Twelve years later my co-writer David Kent and I had a song recorded on a new artist on Giant Records. His name is Blake Shelton, and the song is 'Austin.'

"The first time I heard it was in my co-writer's publisher's office, Talbot Music, who pitched the song and got it cut. The producer, Bobby Braddock, came over to play it for us. By the time it got to the second chorus, I bit my lip thinking, 'I can't sit here and bawl.' I gathered my strength and was able to hold back the tears. A few months later, I was driving by Old Hickory Lake when I first heard it on the radio. I let myself cry then."

- Kirsti Manna
On her first cut, "Austin" by Blake Shelton, which went on to stay at #1 for five weeks, a record for a debut single from a debut recording artist

* * * * *

<u>Kirsti's advice to songwriters</u>:
"Have a plan to pay the bills and still support your songwriting habit. Read the 'Artist's Way'. Do everything you can to open up your creativity. Be objective, but listen to your gut. Most of all, be supportive and happy for others when they are enjoying their success."

NOTES

CHAPTER
11

YOU CO-WRITE ON A REGULAR BASIS
WITH SOMEONE WHO HAS SIGNED
A SINGLE-SONG CONTRACT

YOU CO-WRITE ON A REGULAR BASIS WITH SOMEONE
WHO HAS SIGNED A SINGLE-SONG CONTRACT

Hopefully you'll see the obvious political connection to writing with someone who has signed a single-song contract. They have already established a relationship with at least one publisher who believes in them as a songwriter, and, when your new co-written "song of the year" is done, they will be playing it for that publisher. The publisher, in turn, probably will be interested in who that new co-writer is and may eventually be interested in hearing some of your other songs. But best of all, there's already a new member on your team: there's you, your co-writer, and his publisher (who will be getting your song cut). There can never be too many people working on behalf of your song.

Another less obvious reason is that your co-writer has developed certain writing skills and information that have led to that single-song contract, and you'll be exposed to new thoughts and new techniques in songwriting, making you a better writer. Some people in the business call this "writing up".

An even more subtle reason is what we call the "hope factor". You're in the presence of someone who has done it, and it gives you hope that you can do it too. Writing with someone who is actively succeeding in their pursuits is uplifting and can keep you inspired. If you continue to keep company with unpublished writers who whine and moan about people in the business with window caulking plugging up their ears, you will pick up on a negativity that will only deter your success. It should be an easy choice.

CAUTION: Don't get the wrong idea here. The best co-writers are not necessarily published. The best co-writers are the ones who inspire you and work with you with a sense of teamwork, common purpose and equality. The bottom line is: do you write a great song with your co-writer? Then keep writing with them regardless of whether or not they're published.

Review the techniques in Chapter 3 in searching for co-writers, this time keeping in mind we are now adding the "signed-a-single-song-contract" requirement. Remember those places you listed there that included everything from writer's nights to song classes? Expand that list and keep listening. When you hear someone who inspires you and they happen to mention they just signed a single-song contract with Number One Music, make a note to contact them.

Also, open yourself up to be approached. In Chapters 6 and 9 you have been performing your songs out. Now just because you haven't scored your first published song and someone else has, doesn't mean *you* won't be inspirational to a published writer. She wants to write with you because you have something special. <u>We</u> already know you do, but she has to know it too. When she hears you, she will.

COMMITMENT:
In order to move closer to getting my first cut,
I will co-write on a regular basis with someone who has signed a single-song contract.

_________________________   _________________________________
            Date   Signed

So now, using your well-honed Chapter 3 techniques, you have approached some potential new co-writers. Likewise, you have also been approached by some new potential co-writers. The compliments have been exchanged, the "let's get together sometime" handshakes have been made and the "call me" requests have been vocalized. It's too easy to stop there. Now is the time to follow up.

CO-WRITERS WITH SINGLE-SONG CONTRACTS/APPOINTMENTS

List phone numbers for three NEW potential co-writers with single-song contracts under their belts. Call them and arrange a writing appointment. Make sure both of you are clear as to the place and time of your meeting.

Name: ____
Phone #: _______________________   Email Address: _______________________
Date Called: ____________________   Appointment Date: ____________________
Place: ____

Name: ____
Phone #: _______________________   Email Address: _______________________
Date Called: ____________________   Appointment Date: ____________________
Place: ____

Name: ____
Phone #: _______________________   Email Address: _______________________
Date Called: ____________________   Appointment Date: ____________________
Place: ____

Coming in prepared, especially in a new co-writing situation, is really important here. There's nothing more exasperating than two people sitting in a room for three hours saying, "Whadaya wanna write?" "I dunno, whada you wanna write?" All you'll come up with is a bunch of grammatically incorrect lines.

We know you have napkins from Shoney's with song titles on them, or a song idea you wrote on that scrap 1 by 4 from your part-time trim carpentry job, or some melody ideas you sang into a cassette recorder that's sitting on the nightstand by your bed. Bring them in. Maybe they won't be the song you wind up writing, but they may trigger another even better idea.

NEW SONG IDEAS/TITLES
List below five ideas, song titles or phrases to bring into your next co-writing appointment:

1 ____
2 ____
3 ____
4 ____
5 ____

FINISHED SONG TITLE
When your song is finished, fill in the following:

Title:____

Writers: ____

Date of creation:____

Don't stop now. You've written a great one. You've also made a new friend. If it went well, set up another appointment. Do it again. Keep up the good work. Can you feel it? You're getting closer. We can almost see your name in fine print in parentheses under that song title now. And we're not even squinting.

JV:

After signing my first single-song contract, it was so much easier to write with those who had one under their belts, too. What I didn't realize is how it would make me a better writer. We're like kids with our first taste of the ice cream man's cherry bomb pop. We want more. A songwriter does not live on one single-song contract alone. We were motivated to keep the roll going, write better so another offer would come through. And they did. And that led to more contacts. Gee this is easy! Right.

GH:

I've discovered two important things about co-writing: (1) to co-write with people I like and would have as friends (since you end up spending so much time together) and (2) how important it is for me to be myself. If I can't be comfortable acting like a goof with my co-writer in the room then why bother? It also helps if my co-writer is as goofy as me. And it also helps if they have at least a single-song contract. It tells me they're serious about doing this deal.

* * * * *

From Bob Regan

"I had written a song called 'Routine' which went on to be my first cut by The Kendalls in 1987. I was writing for Dick James Music at the time, and it was pitched by my songplugger to their producer, Ray Pennington. Shortly after, I was listening to a low-watt AM station in Madison,Tennessee when it came on. I did the obligatory pull-over-to-the-side-of-the-road and listened all the way through. I was amazed that not only did I accomplish one of my dreams but that I was actually taking up space on the airwaves."

- Bob Regan
ASCAP award-winning songwriter of such songs as "Till Love Comes Again" by Reba McEntire, "Thinkin' 'Bout You" by Trisha Yearwood and "Soon" by Tanya Tucker

* * * * *

<u>Bob's advice to songwriters:</u>
"Try to find a balance between your instincts and the market, and write to satisfy both of them."

NOTES

CHAPTER
12

YOU HAVE SIGNED A SINGLE-SONG CONTRACT WITH A MUSIC CENTER PUBLISHER

YOU HAVE SIGNED A SINGLE-SONG CONTRACT
WITH A MUSIC CENTER PUBLISHER

This is where that staircase starts getting steeper. In past chapters it's been easy to document taking guitar lessons, scheduling co-writing sessions, even contacting publishers once you've demoed your latest three songs. But you can't hold a gun to a publisher's head and make him sign a single-song contract. Well, actually, we suppose you could, but he still probably wouldn't give you a reversion clause.

If you've reached this point and still haven't signed your first single-song contract, the first thing to do is keep doing what you've been doing -- and that is writing, co-writing, networking, performing and pitching your songs in the major music center of your choice as spelled out in the previous chapters. That's the easy part. The next thing you need to do is <u>write better songs than you've been writing</u>. That's the hard part, but not impossible.

If there's any attitude that you need to carry with you throughout your songwriting career, it is to always strive to get better. If you believe your last composition is a masterpiece, set your sights even higher for the next one. It doesn't always mean you'll accomplish that, but it's worth the effort and will make you a better writer.

Many times landing a single-song contract has a lot to do with luck. Many times it has to do with a great song. And while we can't control how lucky you are or give you a magic formula for writing a great song, we can offer a few suggestions to help you get there.

The first suggestion is write, write, write. The harder you work, the luckier you get. So it makes sense that the more you write, the better songwriter you'll become, and those old worn-out ideas will give way to fresh new ones.

Time after time, we've seen writers make the mistake of having five songs in their catalog for years on end and not only rack up rejection letters, but also not grow as writers. The powers that be in the business like to see writers in it for the long run, and running around with the same old material doesn't show commitment. The publishers you've been so great at contacting constantly want to hear new songs and want to see that commitment in you. When they do, their hands will be closer to bringing out that single-song contract on the desk.

Once that happens, you can expand your publisher network to get more songs signed. But first let's write some more songs.

COMMITMENT:
In order to move closer to getting my first cut,
I will strive to land a single-song contract
by increasing my song catalog and increasing my publisher contacts.

_______________________   _______________________________
        Date   Signed

There are an unlimited number of ways writers build catalog. We personally know successful writers who write 8 songs a year and 5 get cut. We also know writers who write 250 songs a year and 5 get cut. And then there's those who write 25 a year and get 5 songs cut. Your method is your own, and we don't want to try to disrupt that. But for now (remembering we want to increase your catalog) let's set a goal of a minimum of one completed song a month. It doesn't matter if they are solo writes or if there are eight co-writers on one song. Keep in mind this is a minimum and on a per-month basis. If you write 2 songs in August, you are not excused from writing _at least_ one in September.

 ## TRACKING YOUR YEARLY PROGRESS

Here is a chart to help you track your progress throughout the year. Beginning with the next full month first, write in the name of the month (easy), then work as long as it takes that month to complete your hit, (not so easy). Write the song title down and record the date you complete it. Do the same next month, and the next and the next:

Month 1   Song Title   Date Completed
____

Month 2   Song Title   Date Completed
____

Month 3   Song Title   Date Completed
____

Month 4   Song Title   Date Completed
____

Month 5   Song Title   Date Completed
____

Month 6   Song Title   Date Completed
____

Month 7   Song Title   Date Completed
____

Month 8   Song Title   Date Completed
____

Month 9   Song Title   Date Completed
____

Month 10   Song Title   Date Completed
____

Month 11   Song Title   Date Completed
____

Month 12   Song Title   Date Completed
____

By the time this list is filled out next year, we hope you will see that the songs at the end of the list show dramatic improvement. We also hope that publisher will see the same thing and sign one of them. Keep up the good work.

Alright! That contract is signed! Congratulations! But don't reserve a space on your wall for your BMI Song Of The Year award just yet, there's more work to do. Remember, this chapter allows you to rack up some points with additional *different* publishers. Let's go there now.

You now have a stronger foundation on which to expand your publisher base. You have signed a single-song contract. Someone believes in you. They take you and your songs seriously. It's amazing when that happens how others get on the take-you-seriously bandwagon. Let them get on. In fact, let's help them on.

Remember that sales pitch you developed in Chapter 8? Dig it up. We're going to make it better, this time using your new song contract success. Something like this:

"Hi, this is Nick Nasaltone, I've been working with Big Bucks Music and have a single-song contract there and am looking to open some more doors. May I come in and play you some songs?"

REFINING YOUR SALES PITCH

Get out a separate sheet of paper and write down your first draft of your own sales pitch, including the names of the publishers with whom you have signed a single-song contract. Rehearse that sales pitch into a tape recorder just like you did in Chapters 7 and 8. How does it sound? If it needs improvement, do a rewrite. Rehearse again. Once you have the sales pitch that you feel best represents you, write it down here:

____

____

____

____

____

____

PUBLISHER APPOINTMENTS

Get back on the phone (you're well versed in this now, aren't you?) and set up some new appointments. After you've called those new publishers (who are of course anxious to jump on your bandwagon), list all the appointments you have secured here:

Publisher: ____
Date: ____________________________   Time: ____________________

Publisher: ____
Date: ____________________________   Time: ____________________

Publisher: ____
Date: ____________________________   Time: ____________________

Publisher: ____
Date: ____________________________   Time: ____________________

Publisher: ____
Date: ____________________________   Time: ____________________

Before you go in, review those Ten Commandments of Professional Etiquette from Chapter 8.

Have a great meeting and get your signing pen ready.

That's the best we can do for you here. The great song that will really do the trick is up to you. Keep at it. Don't give up. You're getting closer.

JV:

Six months after I had moved to Nashville, I had an appointment with a publisher that had a #1 record on the charts at the time. I got it as a result of a referral from a co-writer of mine (whom I met playing at the Bluebird, by the way). I brought my 3-song tape in, and, as I was sitting there in silence for the first 3 minutes and wondering what she was thinking, I felt my blood pressure and heart rate going through the roof. In spite of that, it was a really pleasant experience. She had some nice helpful comments and even a few compliments. By the time the third and last song began, I knew there wasn't going to be any ASCAP award coming soon, so I relaxed hoping I could just come back again when I had three new songs. Much to my surprise, she offered me a single-song contract on it! It was the same song that had been cut off at the first line by another publisher. (It had a better line this time.) I can't tell you how thrilled I was. Someone in the music business thought my song was special! It was like a rite of passage. A first step on a stone as I was about to cross a turbulent river. I often think about that day and wonder if I would have had the fortitude to stay with it if I hadn't received the encouragement of signing that contract. The song never got cut, but it sure kept me going.

GH:

Every weekend for two years a writer I know (I'll call him "Bob") would diligently get off work on Friday and drive five hours into Nashville, hang out and play writer's nights, then drive another five hours back on Sunday night just making it in time to work Monday morning. His supervisor was used to Bob being tired on Mondays.

Eventually Bob performed in a Sunday night contest in which a publisher had agreed to judge. That performance led to Bob's first single-song contract with the publisher, which eventually led to a staff deal and Bob's first cut, which went top ten.

Bob sleeps in on Mondays now.

* * * * *

From Bruce Channel

"My very first major label cut was on my own record. I recorded 'Hey Baby' in November 1961, and it reached number one in March, 1962. That summer of '62, I was touring England with Delbert McClinton. A new guitar band called The Beatles opened for us. Delbert taught one of their singers, John Lennon, some harmonica licks on that tour. To this day there is a picture on my wall of Delbert and me and the band backstage one night after the show. I still remember their names: John Lennon, Paul McCartney, George Harrison and Pete Best."

- Bruce Channel
BMI award-winning songwriter of such songs as "Stand Up" by Mel McDaniel and "Party Time" by T. G. Shephard, each winning the coveted BMI "Millionaire Award" for recognition of over one million air-plays, and "Hey Baby", which received the BMI "Three Millionaire Award"

* * * * *

<u>Bruce's advice to songwriters</u>:
"Take a page from Mark Twain and say it like people would say it."

NOTES

CHAPTER
13

YOU CO-WRITE ON A REGULAR BASIS
WITH A WRITER WHO HAS
AN EXCLUSIVE SONGWRITING AGREEMENT
WITH A MUSIC CENTER PUBLISHER

YOU CO-WRITE ON A REGULAR BASIS WITH A WRITER WHO HAS AN EXCLUSIVE SONGWRITING AGREEMENT WITH A MUSIC CENTER PUBLISHER

This is one of the really, <u>really</u> big steps. Not as big as actually signing an exclusive agreement, mind you, but still big. Even Ed Sullivan would agree it's really big.

Just like in Chapter 11, when you began writing with single-song contract writers, the political connection is obvious. This time, it's with a writer whose publisher believes in her or his ability so much that they are willing to part with dollars for advances, demos, and even some other expenses. And that publisher is anxious to get a return on her or his investment by working their exclusive writers' song catalogs hard. If you are lucky enough to be in a position to write with an exclusive writer, then obviously that song, if it's a great one, is going to get worked and then worked some more.

But the real reason this is such a big step is that now you are attempting to write with an exclusively published writer who not only focuses his writing relationships with <u>other</u> staff writers, but his publisher also <u>expects</u> it of him. Many publishers actually forbid their staff writers to write with unpublished writers. Not only can there be legal ramifications of dealing with "non-professionals", they don't want their diamonds spending their energy polishing chunks of coal, teaching writing techniques. They want them to write hits with other hit writers. That's what they pay them to do. That's why this step is so big and why it must be taken <u>very</u> carefully.

You just don't walk up to Don Schlitz, four-time ASCAP Writer Of The Year, and say, "Let's write". Not only is he devoting his time to his stable of other staff writers, but he doesn't know you or your abilities. Additionally, if you are an unpublished writer, his outlook is likely that you are still in development and, more importantly, that you don't have a publishing team on your side out there working to get your songs recorded. It's not in his best interest to devote time to you. Not always. But then again, it can be. How?

Your approach lies in building a reputation, just like the staff writers you want to write with did. <u>One way</u> is to rack up your single-song contracts, especially with several different publishers, which is a lot easier than landing a staff position three months after getting off the Greyhound.

<u>Another</u> is to have been lucky enough to land a cut from one of your single-song contracts. But if that already happened you wouldn't be gazing down on these inspirational words right now. You'd be hounding BMI as to when your first royalty check will arrive, only to find out it's a whopping $7.42 (see Chapter 1).

<u>Finally</u>, you could just be writing such great songs that the buzz is all over town about you, and twenty staff writers are lined up on your street honking their horns and screaming, "<u>PLEASE</u> write with me!"

Which of the above scenarios is the most likely for you? Good. We're glad you get it.

Having a stockpile of contracted songs and positive relationships with their publishers will get you closer to those staff writers. As you continue to bring in songs to your circle of listeners, you will soon begin to feel that a few of them are taking an even more serious professional interest in you. That's when you make your request to be hooked up with a staff writer.

The three most common opportunities in which you can make that request are:

1.   You just finished a great song and the publisher you've been working with believes it's a smash. While he is jumping on the table shouting to the world that he has Celine Dion's next #1, you should feel comfortable enough to ask him to set you up with one of his writers. Someone who would complement your abilities. One that he feels would be a good match.

2.   You have a great song idea and have developed it into a verse and chorus with a drop-dead payoff. You feel really stuck trying to get through the second verse. Well, maybe you aren't, but *try* to be for this one. (By the way, you are writing this one by yourself -- see Chapter 2.) Because your publisher relationship is good, you are comfortable playing it for him. (Have we ever mentioned this is a business of relationships? See Chapters 1-12.) If the reaction is positive, confess you're stuck and ask if there is a writer on his staff that would be interested in helping you finish it. We bet your first $7.42 royalty check that there is.

3.   Remember the PRO representative you've been seeing regularly from Chapters 7 and 8? After your latest demo session is mixed and you take it in to him, and he starts the table dance and decides it's time to refer you to Alpha Dog Music, mention you wouldn't mind getting together with some of Alpha's staff writers, too.

Before we get into some exercises, we need to mention that you probably still aren't going to go in and write with Don Schlitz. Not yet. You are going to focus on and be referred to staff writers that are still on their way up. Writers that maybe even haven't had chart success yet, but *do* have the goods to write great songs. The "little guns" as they're sometimes called. But little guns often grow into big guns. It's probably better for you to get together with those little guns anyway because you won't be as intimidated or shy around a "lesser" name. Remember, it doesn't mean they are lesser writers. With any luck, their time is coming, and they will be loading some pretty hefty ammunition of their own. Maybe even with you.

COMMITMENT:

In order to move closer to getting my first cut,
*I will work towards co-writing on a regular basis with a writer
who has an exclusive songwriting agreement with a music center publisher.*

___________________________   ___________________________________
           Date   Signed

CURRENT SINGLE-SONG CONTRACTS

List below every publisher with whom you have signed a single-song contract (minimum of three):

1. ____
2. ____
3. ____
4. ____
5. ____
6. ____

PUBLISHER APPOINTMENTS

Put together a CD or tape of 2 or 3 new songs they haven't heard yet (the ones you are racking up in Chapter 12) and call to make an appointment to play it. Write appointment dates and times here:

Publisher: ____
Date: ____________________________________   Time: ___________________________

Publisher: ____
Date: ____________________________________   Time: ___________________________

Publisher: ____
Date: ____________________________________   Time: ___________________________

Publisher: ____
Date: ____________________________________   Time: ___________________________

Publisher: ____
Date: ____________________________________   Time: ___________________________

 ## GETTING STAFF WRITER REFERRALS

During your publisher appointment, _if_, and only if, the reaction is positive, ask if he might set you up with one of his staff writers, discussing that writer's strengths in melody, lyrics, personality compatibility and if they voted Democrat or Republican. If they agree, they might set up an appointment time or have the writer call you. Try to get them to set up the time. Either way, agree to it, write it in your calendar and, to make us happy, write your new co-writer's name, the date, time and place of appointment here:

Name: ____

Date: ______________________________ Time: _______________ Place: ___________________________

Name: ____

Date: ______________________________ Time: _______________ Place: ___________________________

That was the easy part. Here comes the work.

During your next three-hour solo writing block of time (remember Chapter 2?), start developing some ideas, preferably a lyrical approach with a great payoff. The key here is it has to be different and it has to be special. The old "I hear a melody in your voice" idea isn't going to cut it. CUT it - get it? You need to reach for a "The Song Remembers When" here. Otherwise you will waste this golden opportunity, and guess what? Your new co-writer suddenly doesn't have any more room in his calendar until two years from this October.

GREAT SONG IDEAS/TITLES FOR CO-WRITING

Write down 3 song titles with killer payoff ideas here (be tough on yourself):

1.Title: ____

   Payoff: ____

   ____

2.Title: ____

   Payoff: ____

   ____

3.Title: ____

   Payoff: ____

   ____

⊙ UNFINISHED SONGS FOR CO-WRITING

Also, write down lyrics to 2 unfinished songs with a verse and chorus here (once again, these have to be really great):

Song 1 Title: ____

Verse: ____
          ____
          ____
          ____

Chorus: ____
          ____
          ____
          ____

Song 2 Title: ____

Verse: ____
          ____
          ____
          ____

Chorus: ____
          ____
          ____
          ____

Now you're ready. Don't be intimated, just be prepared. Remember, your new co-writer has walked into that room in your shoes before. We're willing to bet our own $7.42 royalty check that this experience will be uplifting and inspirational. Good luck.

One more thing. It's called gherming. It's acting squirrely and over-doing the compliments, Eddie Haskell style. Don't embarrass yourself by doing it with ANY staff writer. Anytime. Ever.

Hope you're not afraid of heights. Look down and see how far you've come. This pyramid thing isn't so bad after all, is it? You've just completed level three - - "Developing Professional Relationships". You're doing great. Keep climbing.

JV:

Now this one took a little longer in coming. My first appointment with an exclusive writer scared me to death. I almost cancelled, but no, I had a purpose. I knew this was an important step. One of my publishers set it up on my request. I came in armed with ideas, hooks, titles, melodies, verses, choruses, you name it. He didn't like any of them. What he did like was getting to know me and what I was about. And that is what led to our song idea. It's an approach that I use almost all the time now in my co-writing experiences. Thanks for the lesson.

GH:

Jerry was the first person I co-wrote with who has an exclusive songwriting contract. I couldn't have asked for a better first experience. We had already known each other for some time and had a pretty good idea that we'd enjoy writing together. I brought a song idea, and he brought Hot Pockets for dinner.

I often think of events in life being like a game of "connect the dots". Just think, if I didn't move to Nashville or if I didn't work at NSAI or if Jerry wasn't an NSAI evaluator and if we didn't co-write that song together which later led to writing this book together -- then you wouldn't be reading this at this very moment. Cool, huh? (P.S. We never did finish that first song, but we went on to write one even better -- and it's on Jerry's CD!)

* * * * *

From Danny Flowers

"I was honored to have Emmylou Harris be the artist to first record a song of mine. The song was 'Before Believing' and was on the 'Pieces Of The Sky' LP, which was released in the early '70s. The title of the album came from a line in the song, which thrilled me even more.

"I met Emmylou when she was 19 and playing in a bar in Greensboro, North Carolina. We've been great friends ever since. I got a work tape of 'Before Believing' to her, and she recorded it pretty much like I did it on that tape.

"When I first got a copy of the record I was somewhere between exhilarated and terrified. Exhilarated because Emmylou saw fit to sing a song I wrote and terrified because I didn't play the game like everyone else and wasn't sure I could do it again."

- Danny Flowers
ASCAP award-winning songwriter on many songs, not the least of which is "Tulsa Time", recorded by Don Williams and Eric Clapton

* * * * *

<u>Danny's advice to songwriters:</u>
"If you don't please yourself, you won't please anyone else. As far as how to do it, I still don't know how to. I just know there's no right way, and that's what's beautiful about it."

NOTES

CHAPTER
14

YOU HAVE SIGNED AN EXCLUSIVE SONGWRITING
AGREEMENT WITH A MUSIC CENTER PUBLISHER
THAT INVOLVES AN ADVANCE AND A DEMO BUDGET

YOU HAVE SIGNED AN EXCLUSIVE SONGWRITING AGREEMENT WITH A MUSIC CENTER PUBLISHER THAT INVOLVES AN ADVANCE AND A DEMO BUDGET

This is the step that even Ed Sullivan wouldn't be able to describe. Really big doesn't come close. As we discussed in Chapter 13, a staff writer has a publisher who believes in him so much that the publisher is committing time, energy and bucks to get those songs recorded. A publisher who makes that kind of investment is going to do everything possible to get that investment returned. It's in everyone's best interest to get your songs cut, hence the high point value here.

 DEMAND A STAFF WRITING DEAL

Walk in to EMI Music, ask to see the professional manager and demand a staff writing position or else you're going to go to Warner Chappell.

Just kidding.

If you have been diligently writing, pitching, networking, building catalog, "writing up" (see Chapter 11) and nurturing all those relationships step-by-step as we have been mapping out for you in this workbook, the deal may be just around the corner. It may fall right into your lap. Most of the time it doesn't. Most of the time you have to put your lap into a place where that deal will land.

In Chapter 12 we discussed the importance of portraying your commitment to the music business community. You are serious about being a songwriter. It isn't a hobby for you. It's a lifestyle. You'd write songs regardless of whether someone recorded them or not. You'd write because that is not only what you do, but it's who you are. When it is obvious to the powers that be that you have that kind of commitment, coupled with great songs and a talent for writing them, you just might be offered a staff position.

COMMITMENT:

In order to move closer to getting my first cut,
*I will strive to sign an exclusive songwriting agreement as I step up my
commitment profile by further increasing my song catalog and publishing contacts.*

______________________   ______________________________
          Date   Signed

Now, remember in Chapter 12 you committed to completing one song a month? Building even more catalog shows an even greater commitment. Many publishers these days actually require a minimum of 24 songs a year and incorporate a quota into their staff contracts. Let's get there now so you'll be ready when the deal comes:

TRACKING YOUR YEARLY PROGRESS, PART 2

Here is a chart to help you track your progress throughout the year. Beginning with the next full month write in the name of the month, then work as MUCH as it takes that month to complete two songs. Write down the song titles and record the date completed. Do the same the next month, and the next and the next:

Month 1	Song Titles	Date Completed

Month 2	Song Titles	Date Completed

Month 3	Song Titles	Date Completed

Month 4	Song Titles	Date Completed

Month 5	Song Titles	Date Completed

Month 6	Song Titles	Date Completed

Month 7	Song Titles	Date Completed

Month 8	Song Titles	Date Completed

Month 9	Song Titles	Date Completed

Month 10	Song Titles	Date Completed

Month 11	Song Titles	Date Completed

Month 12	Song Titles	Date Completed

Guess what? You are now behaving like a staff writer. Good. One of the staff writer's jobs is to play these songs for her publisher. They have to be heard. Now that you have a regular production schedule, you need to have a regular publisher schedule. Imagine what all those ears will be thinking when every two months you have a new batch of songs to play. A disciplined, committed writer is music to those ears. And we already know that each song is better than the last, so the positive impression you make grows even stronger.

 <u>PITCH-TO-PUBLISHER CALENDAR</u>

Every other month for the next six months you are going to play three or four new songs to all the publishers (a minimum of three) you have been developing relationships with. As in your two-songs-a-month calendar, below is a pitch-to-publisher calendar to fill in. After you have completed your three newest smashes, beginning with the next full month, write in the name of that month, the publishers you set up appointments with and the songs you will play for them. After each appointment, you might also note their response to each song with a word or two (such as pass, love it, keep to listen, etc.). After the six-month period is over, do another six months, and another and another.

Month 1
Publisher #1: ______________________________________
<u>Songs Pitched</u>   Response
1. ____
2. ____
3. ____
4. ____

Publisher #2: ______________________________________
<u>Songs Pitched</u>   Response
1. ____
2. ____
3. ____
4. ____

Publisher #3: ______________________________________
<u>Songs Pitched</u>   Response
1. ____
2. ____
3. ____
4. ____

Month 3
Publisher #1: ____
Songs Pitched   Response
1. ____
2. ____
3. ____
4. ____

Publisher #2: ____
Songs Pitched   Response
1. ____
2. ____
3. ____
4. ____

Publisher #3: ____
Songs Pitched   Response
1. ____
2. ____
3. ____
4. ____

Month 5
Publisher #1: ____
Songs Pitched   Response
1. ____
2. ____
3. ____
4. ____

Publisher #2: ____
Songs Pitched   Response
1. ____
2. ____
3. ____
4. ____

Publisher #3: ____
Songs Pitched   Response
1. ____
2. ____
3. ____
4. ____

Keep this up (and everything you have been doing up to now). Include a few absolutely undeniably great songs, add a touch of good luck, and that deal just might materialize.

You just honored your commitment statement, first, by increasing your song catalog, and second, by increasing your publishing contacts. We can also do more of both by bringing additional co-writers into your songwriting schedule. This will not only help you discipline yourself to be more productive, but it will also increase your visibility with the publishers your new co-writers are working with.

 <u>INCREASING YOUR STABLE OF CO-WRITERS</u>

Add one co-writer (or better yet, two) to your weekly schedule. That puts your writing schedule now to a minimum of 3, maybe 4 times a week. Let's see what your calendar looks like. Show us below your weekly writing schedule by writing the names of your co-writers in the blocks below. Include your sacred solo time, and your co-writing time with previous and new co-writers in the proper spaces. These will include your single-song contract writers and exclusive staff writers you began with in Chapters 11 and 13:

Day of the week	Morning block	Afternoon block	Evening block
Monday	__________	__________	__________
Tuesday	__________	__________	__________
Wednesday	__________	__________	__________
Thursday	__________	__________	__________
Friday	__________	__________	__________
Saturday	__________	__________	__________
Sunday	__________	__________	__________

Now let's review the commitments you have developed through the use of this workbook. If you have skipped any of the chapters to get to this point, your foundation isn't in place, and more than likely you have reached this point with a few bricks still missing. Lets find out which ones those are.

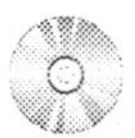 <u>COMMITTMENT REVIEW</u>

Check off:

_____ You solo write regularly.
_____ You co-write regularly.
_____ You do at least one thing each day to further your career.
_____ You've developed industry contacts either by regular visits or by living in a music center.
_____ You have nurtured those contacts into professional relationships.
_____ You perform your songs in a major music center regularly.
_____ You "write up" regularly (co-writers with single-song contracts or exclusive agreements).
_____ You have a stockpile of single-song contracts.
_____ You are writing a minimum of 12 songs per year, reaching for 24.
_____ You strive to make each song better than the last.

Now look at this list. Is everything checked off? Are you being honest with us? And yourself? If not, then go back over the chapters appropriate to the ones you didn't check and go back to work.

If you have truly accomplished everything on this checklist, then keep doing what you're doing and stay with this workbook. Don't give up!

Signing an exclusive songwriter agreement is like getting married. You are both agreeing to a long-term commitment to each other (and if you divorce, the publisher gets full custody of your children). We could write an entire book about considering an exclusive contract. Of course, you'll want to consult your attorney and diligently look over every clause. But there's more to consider. You might want to start playing your songs in work tape fashion, as that is what eventually will be the norm. Can the publisher hear them in that format? Do you like him and the office staff? Your personalities will have ample opportunity to clash now and then. Do you trust them? Make sure your contract addresses accountability on both parties. Do you feel like a member of the family? Not a dysfunctional one, but a positive team-oriented family that lends itself to the mutual benefit of all? Eventually it all comes down to you and how you feel about it. If it isn't right, don't go there. A bad deal is worse than no deal. A great deal will get you your first cut.

JV:

I had been negligent in calling one of my "regular" publishers mainly because after one single-song contract he never took anything again. But he always had the door open for me. Three new songs later, I decided my scars had healed, my skin was a little thicker and it was time to get thrown to the lions again. I called him. Wow, first song he likes. He even played it all the way through. That never happens. Oh my God, he likes the second one too! What does this mean? Even the third one, which I wrote by myself and demoed guitar/vocal on my little 4-track, was to his liking! Next thing I know he tells me they've been looking for a writer to sign in a joint venture with Moe Bandy. It didn't pay much, but was a great opportunity. Was I interested? Is the Pope Catholic? I waited by the phone to hear what Moe would say. I didn't have to wait long. Two days later we were going over the details, and a couple of weeks later contracts were signed. A whopping $50 a week. Sure glad I made that call.

GH:

Not long ago one of my friends was sitting at the reception desk of her full time job wondering why she couldn't get any attention as a writer/artist with the five songs she had written last year. Why wasn't anyone taking her by the hand and leading her to success? One morning she awoke with the idea that maybe she had to put a little more of her own effort into her dream. She got a waitress job at night and spent her days writing and hanging with some "little guns" at a major publishing company, singing on the demos of the songs she wrote with them. A few staff writers in the company heard those demos and asked her to sing on their own demos. A producer in the company got hold of the session and took it in to the head of the company. After some discussion, they offered her a production/writing deal. She still has that waitress job, but now every major label in town is asking about her. Did we mention patience and persistence pay off?

* * * * *

From Roxie Dean

"My first cut was a Christmas song recorded by Reba McEntire. One September, my publisher told me that Reba was doing a Christmas project and I thought it would be pretty cool that if she cut it, we would hear it only a few months later. Lucky for me, she did cut it. The record, however, didn't come out until the <u>next</u> Christmas, a full year later! It was still music to my ears."

- Roxie Dean
Dreamworks recording artist and co-writer of "Why They Call It Fallin'" by Lee Ann Womack and Grammy nominated, "When I Think About Angels" by Jamie O'Neal

* * * * *

<u>Roxie's advice to songwriters</u>:
"Be true to yourself and write what you know. Sometimes your greatest accomplishment comes when you're not looking for it."

NOTES

CHAPTER
15

YOU CO-WRITE WITH
A MAJOR LABEL RECORDING ARTIST

YOU CO-WRITE WITH
A MAJOR LABEL RECORDING ARTIST

99.999% of the time there are scores of people standing in the way between you and a major label recording artist. Their job is to say "pass" on your song without that artist ever hearing your song or even hearing about it. It should be apparent here that writing with a recording artist eliminates all those "nay-sayers".   Well, most of the time.

Yes, you may have a chance to meet Alan Jackson backstage and you may even be foolish enough to hit him up to co-write while he's signing an autograph. At that time he might respond, "Sure, call my manager, we'll set something up", after which he will promptly tell his manager that when you call, to tell you he's on tour in Zimbabwe.

While you may actually have an opportunity to write with a major label recording artist because your uncle is his tax attorney, chances are you won't.   Besides, writing with a major label recording artist is no guarantee it will be cut (see JV comments at the end of this chapter).

The reality is that most recording artists don't have the time to write with established writers, even hit ones, let alone an entry-level writer trying to get their first cut. A better way to look at this is to approach *potential* recording artists. No, you won't get points in this chapter for doing that, but you never know when the day may come and that "potential" recording artist is signing a record deal that you didn't even know was in development. That's when you can rack up your points.

If you're already an established staff writer – one of the "little guns" referred to in Chapter 13- simply call those potential recording artists and/or demo singers and set up an appointment. If that's the case, skip the next paragraph, sign the commitment statement and get to the work afterward. If not, read on.

In Chapters 6, 9 and 10, you have been attending showcases, writer's nights and performing your songs in a major music center. During the course of those activities you have developed relationships (that word again) with certain performers and demo singers who have (hopefully) sometimes complimented your writing. These may all be potential recording artists. If so, chances are they're trying to get a record deal, and that means they'll need hit songs. Our goal in this chapter is to begin writing hits with these potential artists and stay with them until they get a record deal.

COMMITMENT:
In order to move closer to getting my first cut,
I will take steps to co-write with potential and/or major label recording artists.

______________________________   ______________________________
                Date   Signed

SINGERS/CO-WRITERS

Make a list of 5 singers you have heard or have used on demos <u>that you have established a positive relationship with</u>, and with whom you would like to write. Find their phone numbers and list them below:

Singer: _______________________________   Phone Number: _______________________________

Singer: _______________________________   Phone Number: _______________________________

Singer: _______________________________   Phone Number: _______________________________

Singer: _______________________________   Phone Number: _______________________________

Singer: _______________________________   Phone Number: _______________________________

SINGERS/CO-WRITERS APPOINTMENTS

Set up some co-writing appointments with them and mark them in your calendar. Once again, make us happy and write your new co-writers' names, date, time and place of appointments here:

Name: ____

Date: _______________________________ Time: _____________ Place: _______________________________

Name: ____

Date: _______________________________ Time: _____________ Place: _______________________________

Name: ____

Date: _______________________________ Time: _____________ Place: _______________________________

This may look familiar from Chapter 13. And now, just like when you were starting to write with staff writers, we'll continue the process of getting prepared for these new appointments.

Get out your Cracker Barrel napkins, your Home Depot receipts and your bedside tape recorder on which you have written and/or hummed song ideas and/or titles. Be your hardest critic on these ideas, remembering how special they have to be concerning lyrical approach, payoff and melodies. We know you can do it. You've done it before in Chapters 11 and 13.

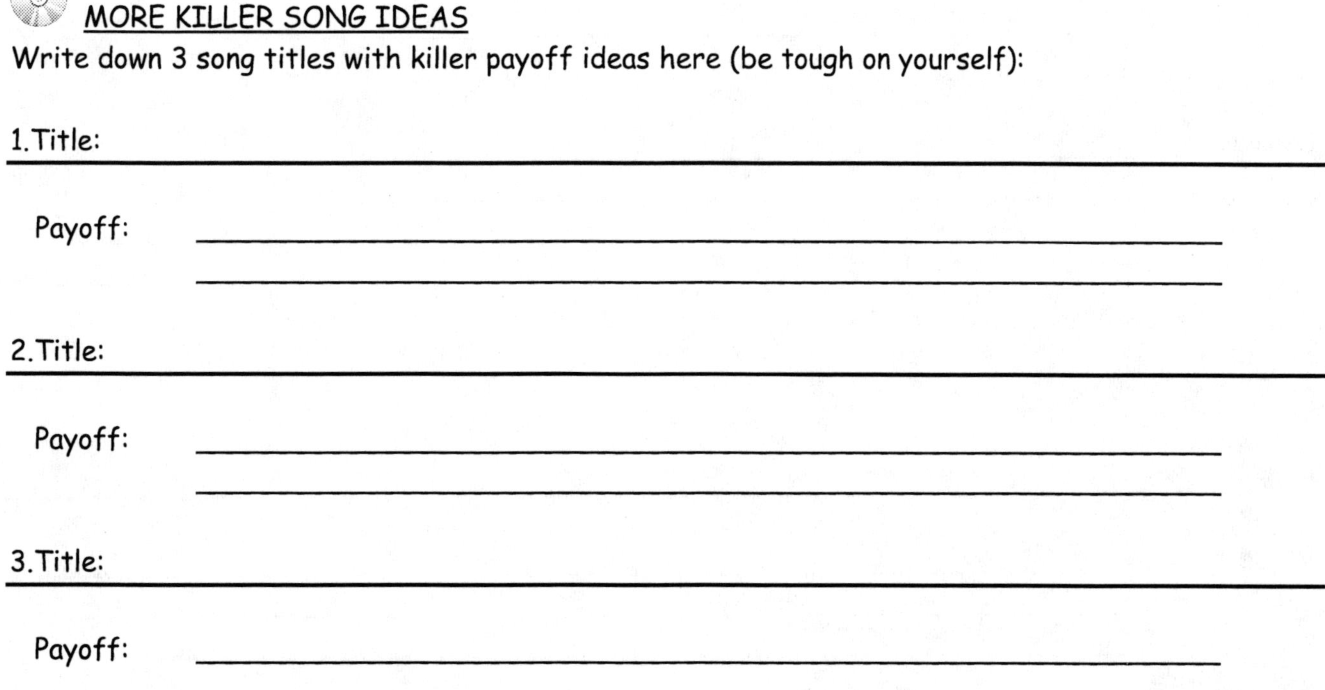

MORE KILLER SONG IDEAS
Write down 3 song titles with killer payoff ideas here (be tough on yourself):

1.Title: ____

   Payoff: ____
               ____

2.Title: ____

   Payoff: ____
               ____

3.Title: ____

   Payoff: ____
               ____

 <u>UNFINISHED SONGS FOR CO-WRITING</u>

Also, write down lyrics to 2 unfinished songs with a verse and chorus here (once again, these have to be really great):

Song 1 Title: ____

Verse: ____
                ____
                ____
                ____

Chorus: ____
                ____
                ____
                ____

Song 2 Title: ____

Verse: ____
                ____
                ____
                ____

Chorus: ____
                ____
                ____
                ____

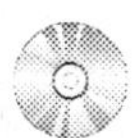 <u>FINISHED SONG</u>

Once you've completed the monster that will get your friend her record deal, write below the song title, your future Academy Award nominee co-writer's name, and the date of the song's creation:

Song Title: ____

Written By: ____

Date of Creation: ____

Just in case you're writing with more than one star:

Song Title: ____

Written By: ____

Date of Creation: ____

Once again, have fun and enjoy this creative process. It's very inspirational to hear a great singer developing a song in progress – especially when it's with you. Again, good luck. You're doing everything right.

You're almost at the top of this pyramid now! Even King Tut didn't get this far. We're proud of you. You've just completed level four - - "Solidifying Professional Relationships". Keep at it.

JV:

The recording artist co-write list is pretty long for me. It includes Joe Diffie, Mike Reid, Lari White, Rob Crosby, Mark Collie, JoAnna Janet, Chalee Tennison, Emerson Drive, Phil Vassar, and Blake Shelton, just to name a few. The cut side of that list is pretty short, that being a song called "Athens Grease" on Phil's second Arista CD, and a new guy on Warner Brothers, Dusty Drake. With any luck, Dusty's record will be out by the time this is in print and he won't be a "new guy" any more.

I've been concentrating my efforts on some "potentials" lately. I am a firm believer in forging these relationships early on. Maybe someday you'll hear the names Julie Burton, Angela Hurt and/or Trenna Barnes. And just maybe a song we wrote will be on their record.

GH:

When I was living in L.A., I co-wrote a song with my singing teacher, John Deaver. John had a student named Jose Miguel who was looking for material to sing. After hearing a song John and I wrote called "Surrender All Night", Jose asked for permission to not only record our song but to translate it into Spanish. We agreed and Jose became a co-writer on the Spanish language version ("Mi Amante Ideal"). Jose is now recording on the Warner Bros. Latin label and recorded "Mi Amante Ideal" for his new CD. I'm told he does backflips on stage. Being that this is my first major-label cut, if I knew how, I'd do backflips too!

* * * * *

From Arlos Smith

"I had written a song with Michael Peterson called 'Love's Great (When You're Not In It).' Shortly after, Michael signed a record deal with Warner Bros. We demoed the song, but it didn't come out quite right and Michael was on the fence about it. I had resigned myself that he wasn't going to cut it, but one night Michael and I were playing a round at the Courtyard Café and I played the song. It revived Michael's interest in it enough to re-demo it, and that demo went on to convince the producers to put it on the record. It was on Michael's debut album. Everyday I look at my first cut on my first gold record framed on my wall and thank my lucky stars that I played that song that night."

- Arlos Smith
Writer of 2000 SESAC Song of the Year "Home To You" by John Michael Montgomery

* * * * *

<u>Arlos' advice to songwriters</u>:
"Write what you feel. If it comes to you at 3 am get up and answer the call."

NOTES

CHAPTER
16

A PUBLISHER HAS DROPPED OFF YOUR SONG TO A MAJOR LABEL A&R REPRESENTATIVE, PRODUCER OR MANAGER

A PUBLISHER HAS DROPPED OFF YOUR SONG TO A MAJOR LABEL A&R REPRESENTATIVE, PRODUCER OR MANAGER

Up until this chapter, we've given you tangible activities to further your chances of getting a cut. These activities were all within your control. You had a choice to do them or not, but the choice was always yours and not someone else's. From here on out you are not quite as in control of your song's destiny as you might like to be.   Someone else is. But remember, *that* someone else is a part of your team and it is also in his/her best interest to get your song cut.

So teamwork is the key here, and that's where your focus will be in this chapter. You've been building a solid foundation. Not only have you been writing your best songs ever, but you've been creating a network and nurturing relationships (stop already!!), especially with publishers who have listened to your songs. We know, we know - - you've heard this relationship stuff again and again, and you're going to hear it yet one more time. Probably more than that. Its importance can't be overstated.

Although dropping off songs to the people that need to hear them may not be as effective as personal appointments, it's still better than your songs not being heard. A song on the shelf only gathers dust. In fact, many listeners in the business will only accept dropped-off songs. And while you may have your doubts, most of them swear that they are openly receptive and listen to everything that comes in. In support of that "receptivity", there are many stories of songs that have been recorded that were merely dropped off at the front desk of a record label.

You're probably asking yourself right now, "Why don't I get questionnaire points for dropping off my hits to someone myself as opposed to a publisher?" Good question. While we don't want to discourage you from doing so, the answer here concerns the *perception of credibility*. The publisher that believes in your song enough to pitch it has developed and nurtured his/her own relationships (there's that "r" word again) with the people who can take your song upstairs. Those people respect your publisher and know that when a song comes to them from him/her, it's worth their time to take it seriously.

Not that they wouldn't take you seriously, but the song has extra clout when it comes in from someone whose reputation precedes them and, as a result, your song, more often than not, has a better chance coming from the publisher. There's a reason why virtually every hit writer has a publisher representing his or her catalog. So go ahead and pitch away, but you'll earn points when a publisher pitches on your behalf.

All that being said, let's get back to your team.

COMMITMENT:
In order to move closer to getting my first cut,
I will keep accurate records of my songs dropped off by publishers.

_______________________   _______________________
            Date   Signed

While you can't force a publisher to pitch your songs, you can (without being an obnoxious pest) gently keep your publisher aware of them and continue to build a positive business relationship between the two of you. We are going to set up a process whereby you will be able to keep track of the publisher's activities regarding your songs. It's important, however, to keep in mind that every publisher has a different attitude about communicating with his writers regarding pitching songs. Some don't like to inform the writer at all, citing that when songs are "passed" on, it may discourage them. Additionally, while a song may be taken by someone, it may unnecessarily get the writer's hopes up. Others like to inform their writers regularly about their pitch activities, thereby letting them know they believe in them and want to keep them encouraged. Most fall somewhere in between. Whatever opinions your publishers may have, honor them.

REVIEWING CURRENT PUBLISHER CONTRACTS/AGREEMENTS
List below every publisher with whom you have a single-song contract and/or an exclusive writing agreement:

<u>Publisher:</u>   <u>Song Title:</u>

____

____

____

____

____

____

____

____

____

____

For every publisher that you've listed <u>two</u> or more songs with, call them and schedule a luncheon appointment. Emphasize that this is not to pitch new songs; it's just to get together. Complete the chart below, listing who the lunch is with, where, when, and what time.

<u>Publisher:</u>   <u>Date:</u>   <u>Time:</u>   <u>Place:</u>

____

____

____

____

____

____

During the course of your luncheon (by the way, you're buying), make an effort to talk about mostly everything <u>except</u> your songs in their company. There's so much to talk about - - How many times is Garth going to retire? The latest awards program. How 'bout them Titans? You get the idea. Sometime during the conversation, the publisher will more than likely bring up what he has been doing with your songs. If he doesn't, casually ask in a positive way, "Have you had any decent response to [your song titles here]?" Remember that it's important to not be a pest. Your publisher will be more responsive to giving you the information you need if he or she doesn't feel under a lot of pressure. That will, in turn, keep your publisher aware of your songs and even generate pitch ideas. And they'll still take your phone calls. For now, DO NOT make pitch suggestions. That will come in time.

PITCH LOG

Record the activities your publisher reports to you and fill in the "Pitch Log" below. The "<u>How</u>" refers to how it was pitched. Was it dropped off or played in person? The "<u>To</u>" section refers to whom it was pitched. Was it to an A&R representative, manager, producer, etc.? If you can, put their names in.   "<u>For</u>" is where you list the intended artist your song is being pitched for. The "<u>Response</u>" column refers to what the reaction to your song was. Was it put on "hold", "kept for listening again later" or "passed" on? You may not know the response (and may never know). In that case, just leave it blank:

PUBLISHER: _________________________________

<u>Song</u>   <u>How</u>   <u>To</u>   <u>For</u>   <u>Response</u>

____

____

____

____

PUBLISHER: _________________________________

<u>Song</u>   <u>How</u>   <u>To</u>   <u>For</u>   <u>Response</u>

____

____

____

____

PUBLISHER: _________________________________

<u>Song</u>   <u>How</u>   <u>To</u>   <u>For</u>   <u>Response</u>

____

____

____

____

Now look at the log you just filled in and go score up some points on your questionnaire.

So that your publisher doesn't feel you're breathing down his neck, wait <u>at least</u> two months before you go through this process again. In fact, we'll be doing this once again two months from now in Chapter 17.

Keeping an accurate pitch log can do more that just get you points for this chapter. Carol Cottonears at Bullet Records may love one of your songs. <u>You have a record of it now</u>. Three months from now, when she's looking for songs for that new band she just signed, you'll remember that and get it pitched again to her. Besides, it's very cool to see tangible progress being made in your songwriting career.

Can you hear it? We can. It's your first cut playing off in the distance.

JV:
It can happen. It was Monday, and Lee Greenwood was supposed to be finishing up his latest album, "Holding A Good Hand". He already had found all of his songs. It was too late to pitch any more. On a whim, however, one of my songs was dropped off to the front desk at Capitol Records on Tuesday. On Thursday I was at my publisher's office writing in a room when he interrupted our session to tell me that Lee was cutting the song that day. Right at that moment, as a matter of fact. It can happen.

GH:
A former A&R representative for a major label once told me about the time he was on a search for songs for one of the label's artists. He took lots of appointments, and at the end of the day he set aside time to listen to the publisher drop-offs that had come to the reception desk. Upon the completion of the project, our A&R friend noticed that, out of the ten songs recorded, four were found by the artist's producer and six were found by him. All six had been dropped off.

---

* * * * *

From Jon Vezner

"My first major label cut was a song entitled 'It's No Secret Anymore' and was recorded by Dave and Sugar on CBS Records in 1985. I was still living in Minnesota at the time and the song was published by Wrensong Music and signed to a single-song contract there.

"I had arrived in Nashville on one of my frequent visits when the record came over to Wrensong and we got to hear it. For the first time someone had recorded my song. Even though Dave and Sugar's career was waning, I can't tell you how excited I was to hear those voices on my tune and to see my name in that little print in parentheses on the record. I remember thinking at the time, 'I'd almost pay to have that happen.' It was an unforgettable moment."

-Jon Vezner
ASCAP award-winning songwriter and co-writer of many hits, including "Where've You Been?" recorded by Kathy Mattea, which went on to receive every major song of the year award, including ACM Song of the Year, Grammy Country Song of the Year, CMA Song of the Year, and NSAI Song of the Year

* * * * *

<u>Jon's advice to songwriters</u>:
"Use the gift God has given you and stay with it. It's what sets you apart. Be fearless."

NOTES

NOTES

CHAPTER
17

A PUBLISHER HAS PLAYED YOUR SONG TO A MAJOR LABEL A&R REPRESENTATIVE, A PRODUCER'S ASSISTANT OR THE MANAGER OF A MAJOR LABEL RECORDING ARTIST

A PUBLISHER HAS PLAYED YOUR SONG TO A MAJOR LABEL A&R REPRESENTATIVE, A PRODUCER'S <u>ASSISTANT</u> OR THE MANAGER OF A MAJOR LABEL RECORDING ARTIST

Here we go again. As in Chapter 16, the control over your songs is still limited. But now, like then, you *can* stay close to them. The reason why the points are higher here is because we're moving up the food chain. Most of the time, playing a song in person seems to achieve more positive results than dropping off a song. Your publisher knows that, so when they're playing your song it will be heard with a little more respect than if it were simply dropped off. Why can't <u>you</u> play them for these people, you ask? Well you can, but you still won't get those questionnaire points for the same reason as in Chapter 16: *credibility*. Also, an A&R representative, etc. is (usually) more comfortable listening to songs from a third party rather than from the writer.

Armed with that knowledge and that which you gained in Chapter 16, let's continue to climb.

COMMITMENT:
In order to move closer to getting my first cut,
*I will keep accurate records of my songs played by a publisher to
a major label A&R rep, producer's assistant, or manager.*

_______________________   _______________________________
        Date   Signed

Two months ago you had a casual lunch with each of the publishers you listed in Chapter 16. During that time you received information about your songs' activities with that company. Now that it's <u>at least</u> two months later, hopefully you have added songs to your catalog and maybe even a publisher or two to your list.

 <u>PUBLISHER PITCH IDEA APPOINTMENTS</u>

Look at your list of publishers in Chapter 16 and update the list if necessary. For every publisher with <u>three</u> or more of your songs, schedule a cup of coffee at the end of a workday. Previously, your lunch was low-key and was not primarily an attempt to hawk your songs. As we're moving up the pyramid, it's now okay to explain that you're hoping to get together with them to go over pitch ideas. Because your lunch two months ago was positive and non-threatening, it's possible the publisher will just make an appointment during the workday to go over those ideas. That's even better - you don't have to buy the cup of coffee. List your appointments below:

<u>Publisher:</u>   <u>Date:</u>   <u>Time:</u>   <u>Place:</u>

____

____

____

____

____

During each meeting you will discuss actions taken regarding your songs. Because you've been doing your homework, you know who's coming up to record and you can suggest certain pitch ideas. Don't forget that Carol Cottonears loved your song two months ago. Oh yeah, about that homework:

<u>PITCH IDEAS</u>

Below is a place for you to organize your pitch ideas for your songs. List your songs and which artists (who are coming up to record) you think they would be good for.

<u>Song Title</u>   <u>Artist(s)</u>

____

____

____

____

____

____

____

Be aware of the fact that the publisher may not agree with some of your pitch ideas. Respect that opinion and go on with your next suggestion. You may feel comfortable enough to ask permission to drop off (or even play, if you can) your pitch idea yourself. Just remember, you don't get questionnaire points for that in this chapter. Go ahead and tell the publisher that your skin is thick and you'd love to know when a pitch is made, if it's okay with him. Remember -- no pressure. That door will start closing quickly when he feels you are pestering him. Pay attention to signals indicating such and also to overtures for you to follow up with him. Be very, very careful.

As the meeting comes to an end, ask permission to get together again in say, two months.

PITCH LOG

Note the activities each publisher reports to you and fill in the Pitch Log below.

PUBLISHER: ___________________________________

<u>Song</u>	<u>How</u>	<u>To</u>	<u>For</u>	<u>Response</u>

PUBLISHER: ___________________________________

<u>Song</u>	<u>How</u>	<u>To</u>	<u>For</u>	<u>Response</u>

PUBLISHER: ___________________________________

<u>Song</u>	<u>How</u>	<u>To</u>	<u>For</u>	<u>Response</u>

This time you found out that Harry Hearingaid, manager for *The Cry-In-Your-Beer Band*, loved your newest up-tempo. Great! Too bad they're not going into the studio until next year, but you'll remember that when they do. Meanwhile, keep those words and melodies coming.

JV:

My co-writer's publisher once played one of our songs to the manager of a new group on Capitol/Universal, an all girl group called Wild Rose (the set-up band to the Dixie Chicks). The manager thought it was great for the group and they worked it up. Next thing we know, it's their second single, a top 20 and a video. Gotta love those managers.

GH:

Sara Light's and Arlos Smith's hit song "Home To You" was first played by Arlos' publisher to the A&R rep at Atlantic Records. He liked the song and put it on a compilation CD along with some other songs and sent that CD to John Michael Montgomery's home. For some time nothing was heard back and Sara and Arlos assumed John passed. One day the phone rang at the publisher's office. It was John calling. He went on and on about how that song was exactly what he was feeling at the time. "Home To You" went on to become the SESAC Song of the Year.

* * * * *

From Kent Blazy

"My first cut was 'Headed For A Heartache' by Gary Morris. I wrote it with Jim Dowell who just happened to play on a softball team with Gary.

"I think hearing your first cut on the radio for the first time is an almost unexplainable feeling. It encompasses so many emotions in those moments. There is joy, excitement, a sense of accomplishment, a thrill of success and the overwhelming thought that you might just be able to make a living doing what you love."

- Kent Blazy
BMI award-winning songwriter of songs recorded by Patty Loveless, Diamond Rio, Clay Walker and, not the least, Garth Brooks, including "If Tomorrow Never Comes". When we asked him, Kent said he has had songs recorded on over 300 billion records. We think it's just a little bit less than that, but not by much.

* * * * *

<u>Kent's advice to songwriters</u>:
"If you can do anything else, do it. If you are totally eaten up by songwriting, listen to as much music of all kinds that you can. Try to hear what makes up a hit song. Read as much as you can. Books about the business give you an understanding of what you are up against. Learn to play as many instruments as you can. Have fun."

NOTES

CHAPTER
18

A PUBLISHER HAS PLAYED YOUR SONG
TO A PRODUCER
OF A MAJOR LABEL RECORDING ARTIST

A PUBLISHER HAS PLAYED YOUR SONG TO A PRODUCER
OF A MAJOR LABEL RECORDING ARTIST

Wow! It's amazing how fast two months go by, isn't it? Your pitch log in Chapter 17 is filled in? Cool. And you've also written four more songs? Great! Don't forget to go back and write them in "Tracking Your Yearly Progress, Part 2" in Chapter 14.

Those A&R reps, producer's assistants, and sometimes even the managers have one main job: to say "no" to the overwhelming number of songs that come their way for their artists. The producer, however, is more focused on looking for songs for the very small handful of artists that he is getting ready to go into the studio with. Playing songs in person to a producer is the next closest thing to getting to the artist. If your publisher is lucky enough to have good relationships with producers, you are one lucky songwriter.

You have gained a wealth of knowledge and communication skills in Chapters 16 and 17 on your climb up this pyramid. Let's go up some more.

COMMITMENT:

In order to move closer to getting my first cut,
I will keep accurate records of my songs played by a publisher to a producer.

___________________________   ___________________________________

       Date   Signed

MORE PUBLISHER PITCH IDEA APPOINTMENTS

Go back to your publisher's list in Chapter 16 and update it if necessary. For every publisher with <u>five</u> or more of your songs, call and ask for an appointment to come in and share pitch ideas for upcoming projects. List your appointments below:

<u>Publisher:</u>   <u>Date:</u>   <u>Time:</u>   <u>Place:</u>

____

____

____

____

____

 ## <u>MORE PITCH IDEAS</u>

Remember how you've done your homework regarding who's looking, when they're cutting, and who's producing them? Fill in your pitch ideas in the chart below:

<u>Song Title</u>	<u>Artist(s)</u>	<u>Producer</u>	<u>Cutting Date</u>

During each meeting you will discuss actions taken on your songs and suggest the pitch ideas you've listed above. You might want to note that Harry Hearingaid, manager of The Cry-In-Your-Beer Band, loved that uptempo of yours and that you heard Ivan Iknowahit is producing them. Maybe it's a good pitch idea for when your publisher has that appointment with Ivan.

PITCH LOG

Note the activities each publisher reports and fill in the Pitch Log below:

PUBLISHER: ________________________________

Song   How   To   For   Response

____

____

____

____

PUBLISHER: ________________________________

Song   How   To   For   Response

____

____

____

____

PUBLISHER: ________________________________

Song   How   To   For   Response

____

____

____

____

Looking at the above log, note when a song is played to a producer. Rack yourself up some points!
You are getting sooooooo close! Keep up the great attitude.

JV:

One of my co-writer's publishers played our song to Jo Dee Messina's producer. He didn't hear it for Jo Dee. No, he heard it for Tim McGraw. God bless him. The publisher, the producer and Tim.

GH:

Sandy Ramos co-wrote a song called "Let Her Rip" with Billy Crain, who had just signed a publishing deal with Paul Worley. Paul was in the midst of producing Martina McBride. Billy played the song to Paul with Martina in mind. Paul heard it instead for a new act -- some group called the "Dixie Chicks".   Over ten million records later they sure are "some group".

* * * * *

From Karen Taylor-Good

"My first major label cut began on a funny journey. After I had finished co-writing 'How Can I Help You Say Goodbye,' I was certain it was the song that would bring about the record deal I had been working so hard to get. I started playing it out all over Nashville hoping to be heard.

"Paul Worley was familiar with the song and one day while in the studio with Pam Tillis, he called asking if Pam could cut the song for her newest project. It was my song, so brilliant me said 'no.' Meanwhile my SESAC rep in New York dropped it off to Atlantic's A&R department where that and some of my other songs were heard. The head of Atlantic called Warner Chappell Music and eventually we struck a staff deal.

"Soon after, Patty Loveless wanted to record it, and I still wanted it for me. My publisher (thankfully) overruled my objections and Patty made it a great record. As she did, I said, 'There goes my song,' thinking my artist career was over.

"There goes my song. Straight into a Grammy nomination and a CMA nomination for Song Of The Year. I'm now making my own CDs and recording songs I love as much as I love 'How Can I Help You Say Goodbye.'

Thank you Patty."

-Karen Taylor-Good
Grammy nominated, CMA nominated and SESAC award-winning songwriter

* * * * *

<u>Karen's advice to songwriters</u>:
"Be vulnerable. Be real. Don't try to be what you're not. If it's supposed to happen, it will."

NOTES

CHAPTER
19

AN A&R REP, ARTIST MANAGER, OR A PRODUCER
HAS PLAYED YOUR SONG
TO A MAJOR LABEL RECORDING ARTIST

AN A&R REP, ARTIST MANAGER, OR A PRODUCER HAS
PLAYED YOUR SONG TO A MAJOR LABEL RECORDING ARTIST

On those rare, wonderful, and miraculous moments when one of the above loves your song enough to play it for an artist, it's not yet time to celebrate a cut but it <u>is</u> time to rejoice in the fact that you didn't hear that four-letter word - "pass" - right away. Usually the process is that the A&R rep, manager, or producer collects songs they like, puts them on a compilation CD and schedules a meeting with the artist, informing them that these are the songs they've looked long and hard to find for them. Often they will go in with a bit of a sales pitch of their own to the artist as to why these are great songs and are worthy of the artist recording them. While it's no guarantee the artist will cut them, it's a great shot.

COMMITMENT:

In order to move closer to getting my first cut,
I will keep accurate records of my songs
played by A&R reps, producers, or managers to a major label artist.

______________________   ______________________________
               Date   Signed

EXPANDED PITCH LOG

Go back to your pitch logs in Chapters 16, 17 and 18 and note in the response column if any songs were kept to play to their artists. Fill in the chart below noting the song title, the name of the representative, the artist it was intended for, if it was played for the artist and if so, what the artist's response was.

<u>Song Title</u>	<u>Representative</u>	<u>Artist</u>	<u>Played For Artist?</u>	<u>Artist's Response</u>

 ## PUBLISHER PITCH IDEA MEETING

You may not know if the song was played for the artist and, moreover, what the artist's response was. If that's the case, and if it's been at least two months since your last publisher meetings, schedule some more and tell us about them below:

<u>Publisher:</u>   <u>Date:</u>   <u>Time:</u>   <u>Place:</u>

____

____

____

____

____

PITCH IDEAS

Below is a place for you to organize your pitch ideas for your songs. List your songs and which artists (who are coming up to record) you think they would be good for.

<u>Song Title</u>   <u>Artist(s)</u>

____

____

____

____

____

____

By the way, as you and your publisher are becoming more comfortable with each other, you may combine your "new songs meeting" (you have four more, right?) with your pitch ideas. During this meeting, ask your publisher if he has heard back from that rep who loved your latest love ballad. Your publisher may know everything that happened with the song, and if it was played and even the artist's response. If not, sometimes this triggers the publisher to do a follow up and let you know. Either way, if you have gathered any information, fill it in the expanded pitch log above. If a song has been played, give yourself those precious points. If not, let it go. Good news will have a way of finding you.

JV:

I've lost count of how many times this has happened. At least I know the artist heard it, and it's pretty cool when someone thinks enough of your song to stake his or her reputation on it. Although it wasn't my song, my publisher pitched one of her other writer's songs to an A&R rep. She went on to play it to their flagship artist. He passed. The A&R rep didn't lose faith in the song and played it for a new artist on the roster. Some guy named Blake Shelton. The song was called "Austin".   Five weeks at #1. I can't help but wonder what that "flagship" artist was thinking when it went to the top – and stayed there - for Blake.

GH:

Once an A&R rep had collected several songs for his artist about to begin his new record. The rep was very excited about several of the songs he found and was anxious to play them. The artist arrived at the meeting and, being in a very unreceptive mood, began passing on everything that came up. After he could contain his frustration no longer, our A&R hero let the artist know that he worked very hard to find these songs and that the artist needed to get the cotton out of his ears. The next song that came up went on hold and then was cut. Now that's what I call a sales pitch.

* * * * *

From Layng Martine, Jr.

"My first cut after moving to Nashville was a song called 'I Don't Want To Be A One Night Stand.' It was around 1972/3 and I was writing for Ray Stevens at the time. When I played the song for Ray, he loved it and called his friend Chet Atkins to set up an appointment for me to play it for him. We didn't even have a demo at the time so Ray and I went over to Chet's office and I played it on my guitar. Chet's response was simple, 'I think I'd like to record that on Jessi Colter.' Jessi had yet to record 'I'm Not Lisa,' but I knew her as a great singer as well as Waylon Jennings' wife so I was very excited about her doing it.

"I actually got to hear it right after it was recorded and while I was deliriously happy, I was even more ecstatic that Chet Atkins and Ray Stevens actually liked one of my songs.

"In the early seventies, country radio had huge playlists and it was a miracle to hear one of your songs unless it was a big hit. 'I Don't Want To Be A One Night Stand' reached only the bottom of the charts, but I got to hear it and it was a wonderful experience. Ironically, the same song later became Reba McEntire's very first single and again got into the 80s on the charts."

- Layng Martine, Jr.
Award winning songwriter of such classics as Elvis Presley's "Way Down", Billy Crash Craddock's "Rub It In" and Reba McEntire's "The Greatest Man I Never Knew"

* * * * *

<u>Layng's advice to songwriters</u>:
"Loving songwriting and needing to do it is your greatest asset."

NOTES

NOTES

CHAPTER
20

A PUBLISHER HAS PLAYED YOUR SONG
TO A MAJOR LABEL RECORDING ARTIST

A PUBLISHER HAS PLAYED YOUR SONG TO A MAJOR LABEL RECORDING ARTIST

Do we even need to mention the benefit here? Do you see any A&R people, assistants, interns, managers, producers, ex-wives, receptionists, lawyers, accountants, publicists, hairdressers, personal trainers, dog sitters or _anyone_ with an opinion getting in between your song and the artist? That's the point. There aren't any. This is the best-case scenario, and if you are one of the lucky ones to have your song played directly to an artist via your publisher, you are in a small but privileged minority. When it happens, pinch yourself to make sure it's real.

> **COMMITMENT:**
> In order to move closer to getting my first cut,
> *I will keep accurate records of my songs played by a publisher to a major label artist.*

_______________________   _______________________________
            Date   Signed

ARTIST PITCH LOG
Go back to your pitch logs in Chapters 16, 17 and 18, and note in the response column if any of your songs were played by a publisher to a major label artist. Fill in the chart below noting the song title, the name of the publisher, the artist it was played for, if the artist responded and what the artist's response was.

Song Title	Publisher	Artist	Artist's Response

If you are able to fill in even one line above, give yourself those points. If not, be patient, keep writing and keep up the good work. But we don't really need to tell you that. If you've made it this far - you already know.

You should be retrieving the above information in the regular song and pitch idea meetings you are having with your publisher about every two months. Keep in mind you are not a pest. Don't be calling for meetings every other week. Your publisher will appreciate that and it will pay off for you in the long run. Give him at least 2 months to give you your information.

Congratulations on completing level five - - "Professional Relationships Working For You".

There's a CD in the very near future with your song on it. There's a name below that song title. It's tiny, and it's in parentheses, but it's yours. And you earned it.

Hang in there.

JV:

Tim McGraw was a struggling artist at the time. His first album didn't do zilch. His last single topped out somewhere in the forties. He was hungry for songs and wasn't getting them. I had played a song to Tim's producer for that first project and it was passed on. My publisher was an old friend of Tim's, so Tim came in one day looking for a hit. My publisher played Tim that same song and Tim said, "Put that one on hold. No, put it on cut!" When I was asked if I wanted a Tim McGraw cut, I said "Sure, why not?" It went on the "Not A Moment Too Soon" CD. Now it's five and a half million records later. Sure, why not? There's absolutely no reason why not.

GH:

When Roger Dillon wrote "Sticks and Stones" he had then-unsigned singer Tracy Lawrence come over and sing the demo for him. When Tracy finished, he collected his $40 demo fee, and told Roger, "When I get a deal, I'm going to record that song." Roger didn't hold his breath, but Tracy kept his word. Not only was it Tracy's debut single and his breakthrough record going straight to #1, "Stick and Stones" was the set-up for his debut double platinum album. Roger made his $40 back and then some.

---

* * * * *

YOU WRITE A SONG
Writers: Gracie Hollombe and Jerry Vandiver

When the one you love doesn't love you back
And you toss and turn at three in the morning
And you hear a train cross a distant track
There in the dark some words start forming
And you write a song

    Maybe it'll make the night easier to get through it
    Maybe it'll ease the pain but that's not why you do it
    It's not a temporary, momentary, ordinary passion
    You write a song because you have to

When it's Monday morning and a dollar and change
Is all you've got to make it to Friday
And then the car breaks down in the passing lane
And waitin' for the tow – well you could start cryin'
But you write a song

    Maybe someday down the road you'll hear it on your hometown station
    Or maybe gold will grace your wall but that's not your motivation
    It's not a temporary, momentary, ordinary passion
    You write a song because you have to

Something reaches down to the core
And then something's there that wasn't there before

    And maybe it'll still live on long after you leave here
    Or maybe it'll change a life but that's not your reason
    It's a grip your soul, won't let go, extraordinary passion
    You write a song because you have to

* * * * *

NOTES

A Parting Thought

After the devil lost his prized golden fiddle down in Georgia, he was in a very bad mood. He needed to get a soul fast so he could save face. He set his sights on a guy in Missouri, and called in his three best demons. He told each demon to come up with a plan to get this Missouri guy's soul. The one with the best plan would have the honor of nailing him.

After much thought, each demon approached the devil with his plan.

The first demon said, "I will poison his soul with the temptation of money."

The devil rebuked him saying, "This man has no weakness for material possessions and riches. You cannot have him."

The second demon said, "I will lure him with the temptation of women and infidelity."

The devil replied, "This man loves his wife unconditionally and would never yield. You cannot have him."

The third demon said, "I will discourage him."

The devil said, "Go get your man."

APPENDIX

Academy of Country Music
6255 Sunset Blvd., #923
Hollywood, CA 90028
(323) 462-2351

www.acmcountry.com

Academy of Motion Picture Arts and Sciences
8949 Wilshire Blvd.
Beverly Hills, CA 90211
(310) 247-3000

www.oscar.org

American Songwriter Magazine
1009-A 17th Avenue S.
Nashville, TN 37212
(800) 739-8712 (615) 321-6096

www.americansongwriter.com

ASCAP
7920 W Sunset Blvd, 3rd floor
Los Angeles, CA 90046
(323) 883-1000

www.ascap.com

ASCAP
2 Music Square West
Nashville, TN 37203
(615) 742-5000

ASCAP
One Lincoln Plaza
New York, NY 10023
(212) 621-6000

ASCAP has additional offices in Atlanta, Chicago, London, Miami and Puerto Rico

The Bluebird Café
4104 Hillsboro Rd.
Nashville, TN 37215
(615) 383-1461

www.bluebirdcafe.com

BMI   www.bmi.com
8730 Sunset Blvd.
Los Angeles, CA 90069
(310) 659-9109

BMI
10 Music Square East
Nashville, TN 37203
(615) 401-2000

BMI
320 W. 57th St.
New York, NY 10019
(212) 586-2000

BMI also has offices in Atlanta, Miami, London and Puerto Rico

CMJ Network   www.cmj.com
151 W 25th St., 12th Flr.
New York, NY 10001
(917) 606-1908

Country Music Association (CMA)   www.cmaworld.com
One Music Circle South
Nashville, TN 37203
(615) 244-2840

Gospel Music Association   www.gospelmusic.org
1205 Division St.
Nashville, TN 37203
(615) 242-0303

International Music Products Music Association (NAMM)   www.namm.com

Jerry Vandiver   www.jerryvandiver.com

Just Plain Folks   www.jpfolks.com

LA Weekly   www.laweekly.com
6715 Sunset Blvd.
Los Angeles, CA 90028
(323) 465-9909

Los Angeles Convention & Visitors Bureau   www.lacvb.com
633 W Fifth St. Suite 600
Los Angeles, CA 90071
(213) 624-7300

Los Angeles Tourist Information   http://losangeles.citysearch.com

Midem International Music Conference   www.midem.com

Muse's Muse   www.musesmuse.com

Music Connection Magazine   www.musicconnection.com
4215 Coldwater Canyon
Studio City, CA 91604
(818) 755-0101

Music Industry News Network (Mi2n)   www.mi2n.com

Music Row Magazine   www.musicrow.com
1231 17th Ave. South
Nashville, TN 37212
(615) 321-3617

Nashville Convention & Visitors Bureau   www.nashvillecvb.com
211 Commerce St., Ste. 100
Nashville, TN 37219
(615) 259-4700

Nashville Scene   www.nashvillescene.com
2120 8th Ave. South
Nashville, TN 37204
(615) 244-7989

Nashville Songwriters Association International (NSAI)   www.nashvillesongwriters.com
1701 West End Ave., 3rd Floor
Nashville, TN 37203
(800) 321-6008

Nashville Tourist Information   http://nashville.citysearch.com

National Academy of Popular Music   www.songwritershalloffame.org
330 W. 58th St., Suite 411
New York, NY 10019
(212) 957-9230

National Academy of Recording Arts & Sciences   www.grammy.com
3402 Pico Blvd.
Santa Monica, CA 90405
(310) 392 3777

National Academy of Recording Arts & Sciences
1904 Wedgewood Ave.
Nashville, TN 37212
(615) 327-8030

National Academy of Recording Arts & Sciences
156 West 56th St., 17th Flr.
New York, NY 10019
(212) 245-5440

New York City Visitor Information Center   www.nycvisit.com
810 Seventh Ave
New York, NY 10019-5818
(212) 484-1222

New York Tourist Information   http://newyork.citysearch.com

Performing Songwriter Magazine   www.performingsongwriter.com
P.O. Box 40931
Nashville, TN 37204
(615) 385-7796

Radio And Records Magazine   www.rronline.com
1106 16th Ave. South
Nashville, TN 37212
(615) 244-8822

The Rage Entertainment Guide   www.nashvillerage.com
1221 17th Ave. South
Nashville, TN 37212
(615) 664-2270

SESAC, Inc.   www.sesac.com
501 Santa Monica Blvd. #450
Santa Monica, CA 90401
(310) 393-9671

SESAC, Inc.
55 Music Square East
Nashville, TN 37203
(615) 320-0055

SESAC, Inc.
421 W. 54th St.
New York, NY 10019
(212) 586-3450

Songwriters Guild of America (SGA)   www.songwriters.org
6430 Sunset Blvd., #705
Hollywood, CA 90028
(323) 462-5430

Songwriters Guild of America
1222 16th Ave. South, #25
Nashville, TN 37212
(615) 329-1782

Songwriters Guild of America
1560 Broadway, #1306
New York, NY 10036
(212) 768 7902

Songwriter Universe   www.songwriteruniverse.com

South By Southwest Music Conference, Austin, TX   www.sxsw.com

TAXI   www.taxi.com

The Music Business Registry   www.musicregistry.com

U.S. Copyright Office   www.lcweb.loc.gov/copyright/
101 Independence Ave. S.E.
Washington, DC 20559-6000
(202) 707-3000

Women In Music, Inc.   www.womeninmusic.com
31121 Mission Blvd., #300
Hayward, CA
(510) 232-3897

Women In Music in New York
(212) 459-4580

Your First Cut   www.yourfirstcut.com